# Investing in Multifamily Real Estate

A Guide to Investing for Income,
Impact, and Generational Wealth

Maria L. Ellis, BBA, MBA

Washington, DC, USA



Published 2025

DISCLAIMER

# ADVANCE PRAISE

"Through my years in the industry it has always been about buying and selling, but true wealth generation is in buying and holding. This book brilliantly bridges the gap between income, impact, and growth. A blueprint for investors who want both returns and purpose."

— Ure R. Kretowicz, Chairman of the Board & CEO | The Cove Equity Group LLC, USA

"Finally—a guide that doesn't just show you how to invest, but why it matters. Smart, strategic, and deeply purposeful."

— Jayant Davar Chairman, Managing Director & CEO of Sandhar Technologies, India

"Grounded in experience and rich with actionable advice. A must-have manual for those ready to scale their portfolio with confidence."

— Charles Rothschild, UOL.com/Brazil

"A thoughtful and comprehensive guide that empowers readers to take control of their financial future while creating community value."

— Barry Akrongold, Fortune Financial LLC, USA

"An invaluable resource for multifamily investing. This book is a must read for anyone serious about understanding the dynamics of multifamily investing and building generational wealth"

— Mykeal Pitts – Primrose Group, USA

# TABLE OF CONTENTS

# FOREWORD

Multifamily real estate is one of the most powerful vehicles for building wealth, and like any serious business, it demands clarity, discipline, and execution.

Too many people get stuck grinding. Trying to scale by buying one single-family home at a time, answering every tenant call, handling every repair, and wondering why their income and lifestyle doesn't match the hours they're putting in. That approach isn't sustainable, and it certainly doesn't build real freedom.

Maria Ellis gets that. And in this book, she lays out a clear, actionable roadmap for investors who are ready to make the shift from hustle to scale, from chaos to control, from theory to results.

What I appreciate most is that this book isn't fluff. It doesn't sell pipe dreams. It's built on real deals, real numbers, and real experience. Maria combines her background in banking and global finance with years of hands-on investing to give you a complete framework for doing this the right way.

She walks you through every stage of the process, from defining your investor identity and underwriting deals to raising capital, managing risk, scaling operations, and exiting with intention. And she does it with a level of professionalism and clarity that this industry needs more of.

If you're serious about building income, impact, and generational wealth through multifamily real estate, this book will show you how to do it. Not by guessing. Not by grinding. But by following a proven strategy—and surrounding yourself with the right people to get it done.

This is a business. Treat it like one. Read this book, then take action.

**Ken Gee**
Founder & Managing Member|
KRI Partners

# CHAPTER 1:
# STUCK IN THE GRIND: THE INVESTOR WITH BIG DREAMS BUT LIMITING BELIEFS

*"Your limiting beliefs are the only thing standing
between you and the wealth you were meant to create.
Let go of the grind – build with purpose, partner
with power, and rise with intention."*

— Maria L. Ellis

If you've picked up this book, it's likely because you've been asking yourself a simple but powerful question: "Isn't there a better way to escape the 24/7 landlord grind?"

You may be like Frank. Frank always wanted to spend more time with the kids and enjoy fun vacations with his wife and family. He wasn't new to the game – he had bought, renovated, rented, and sold single-family homes for years. He knew how to hustle, how to add value, and how to close deals. But the work? Exhausting. The returns? Modest. The lifestyle? Overwhelming.

Frank was doing everything himself – every decision, every late-night call from tenants, every contractor who didn't show up. He took pride in being the one who could handle it all, the steady hand in the chaos. But that pride slowly turned into exhaustion. And as the cracks began to show, so did something he hadn't expected: a deep, disorienting sense of loss. If he wasn't the tireless problem-solver, the one who always pushed through – then who was he? When the hustle stopped working, so did the version of himself he'd spent years building.

One day, I offered him a different perspective. "What if you shifted to multifamily investing?" I said. "Start small – maybe a ten-unit property. Build a support team. Learn to leverage other people's strengths and capital."

Frank was skeptical. He had doubts. He took pride in being hands-on, but underneath the surface, burnout was setting in fast. And with it came the voice he couldn't quite silence: *"No one else will do it right. If I let go, everything will fall apart. I'm the only one who can keep this thing running."* These weren't just passing thoughts – they were limiting beliefs that had taken root over years of grinding. He didn't just fear delegating; he feared what it would mean about him if he stopped doing it all. Without the hustle, who was he?

But here's the truth: multifamily real estate is how real scale and freedom are built. It's not about doing more work – it's about doing smarter work with the right people around you. Once Frank made that mental shift, his entire investment journey changed.

"If you see yourself in Frank, you're not alone."

Maybe you've been grinding for years, buying one property at a time, hoping the next deal will be "the one." You're putting in the hours, but your income isn't compounding. Your freedom isn't growing. And worst of all – you're doing it alone.

If that resonates with you, you're not just in the right place. You're right on time.

This book is written for you – the driven real estate investor who's ready to level up, who's tired of spinning their wheels, and who knows, deep down, there has to be a more strategic, sustainable path.

You don't need to be rich to start. You don't need to be perfect. You just need to shift your mindset, surround yourself with the right people, and commit to thinking bigger. That's what we'll walk through together, step by step.

So, stop grinding and start building – not alone, but with the right people beside you. That's where real wealth begins. Let's go. Turn the page – and let's start building a future defined by income, impact, and generational wealth.

# CHAPTER 2:
# MY JOURNEY FROM BANKER TO MULTIFAMILY INVESTOR

*"Don't be afraid to start over. It's a chance
to build something better this time."*
— Unknown

After spending two decades in banking – first with Bank of America and later with Citibank – I had helped corporations move billions of dollars across borders, navigate complex markets, and access large seven-figure lines of credit. My career had been defined by financial strategy, global relationships, and high-stakes transactions – but nothing captured it more than the day a $2.3 billion deal with PEMEX nearly collapsed over a single missing clause. I still remember sitting in a Mexico City boardroom, the air thick with tension, as legal teams scrambled, and the clock ticked toward a hard deadline. Billions were on the line, and one misstep could have sent years of work into freefall. In the final hour, I stepped in to mediate between the parties, reframed the clause, and helped broker a solution that satisfied both sides. The deal closed.

It was a powerful reminder that, in any deal – whether you're structuring a multinational energy agreement or acquiring a 230-unit apartment complex – the ability to stay calm under pressure, communicate clearly, and solve problems creatively is what ultimately drives success. Those same principles now guide every decision I make in multifamily investing.

But after years of serving high-net-worth clients and multinational firms, I realized I wanted to build something of my own. I wanted tangible, lasting impact. That desire led me to real estate. I began my real estate journey by helping others – advising clients on residential and commercial properties in Manhattan, where I facilitated several seven-figure deals. Many of my clients were international investors who trusted my financial acumen and cross-border experience. But as I guided them through property acquisitions, I saw an opportunity for myself as well. I began investing personally – first in residential properties, then exploring the multifamily space.

Back then, I wasn't just like Frank – I was the one standing on the sidelines, advising others as they built the kind of wealth I only dreamed about. I believed in real estate. I had seen firsthand how it created lasting financial legacies for my clients. But when it came to multifamily investing for myself, I felt stuck. It seemed like a world reserved for institutions or people with deep pockets and insider access. I told myself, "Maybe it's too late. Maybe this game isn't meant for someone like me."

But with the help of real estate coaching, I began to see things differently. I started asking better questions, surrounding myself with people who had done it before, and challenging the limiting beliefs that kept me small. That's when everything began to shift – from watching others build, to finally building something of my own.

The more I studied my clients' moves, the more I realized: multifamily real estate is a team sport. It's not about doing everything yourself. It's about building a network, identifying the right opportunities, and aligning with the right partners. So, I made a decision. I wasn't just going to advise others on their investments – I was going to become a buyer myself.

I began by analyzing properties not just as a consultant, but as a potential owner. One of my first deep dives was a ninety-six-unit property in Queens, New York, where I spotted under-market rents and an expiring loan that gave me leverage. I negotiated a seller credit for deferred maintenance, secured below-market financing, and structured the deal to allow for cash-out refinancing within eighteen months. I wasn't just looking at numbers anymore – I was looking for ways to create value, stabilize rents, and unlock hidden upside with terms that worked in my favor.

The process felt familiar, yet entirely different. I was still solving problems, managing risk, and maximizing returns – but now, I could walk the property, talk to tenants, and witness the transformation unfold in real time. I had a front-row seat not just to their deals, but to their discipline. Over and over, I saw the same pattern: the wealthiest clients weren't chasing trends or gambling on the next big thing – they were consistently investing in multifamily real estate.

And they weren't relying on luck. They were building wealth through repeatable, intentional habits: underwrite one deal every day, make three offers a week, review financials every Friday, walk your properties monthly, and never stop refining your systems. These routines weren't flashy – but they were powerful. They created momentum, clarity, and compounding returns. I realized wealth wasn't built in leaps. It was built in layers – habit by habit.

So, I began building my own. I set aside two hours each morning to study deals, track markets, and reach out to brokers – no excuses. That single habit changed everything. It shifted me from observing success to actively creating it.

Eventually, I learned the secret: scale matters. Buying more than a hundred-unit properties wasn't just for the elite – it was possible with the right mindset, the right partners, and the right structure. I started assembling my own team. I partnered with people whose skills complemented mine – analysts, asset managers, capital raisers, and construction specialists. Together, we were stronger. We moved faster. We created real value.

Today, I invest not just for income, but for impact and generational wealth. And you can too.

This chapter isn't about theory – it's about what's truly possible when you take the first step, even without having all the answers. My journey is proof that you don't need to have it all figured out from the start. You just need the courage to begin, the humility to keep learning, and the wisdom to surround yourself with the right people. Everything else grows from there.

So, ask yourself: what's one small step you can take today to move closer to the investor – and the life – you want to become? Start there. The rest will follow.

# CHAPTER 3:
# UNDERSTANDING THE
# REAL ESTATE LANDSCAPE

*"Real estate is not just about property*
*– it's about possibility."*
— Maria L. Ellis

Real estate is a vast and varied landscape – full of possibilities, pitfalls, and opportunities for transformation. From single-family rentals and luxury condos to multifamily buildings and commercial assets, each type of investment offers unique rewards and risks. And the investors who succeed are the ones who choose their lane with clarity and purpose.

In this chapter, we'll explore the different real estate asset classes, break down their pros and cons, and help you see where multifamily fits into the bigger picture. Start by getting honest about your current position – your resources, your risk tolerance, and the vision you're working toward.

When most people think of real estate, they picture buying a house and renting it out or renovating and selling it for profit. While this is one entry point, the real estate industry is far broader, with a range of asset classes, investment strategies, and risk profiles.

Understanding this landscape is critical – because choosing the wrong asset type or strategy can slow your growth, drain your resources, or burn you out. But when you align your goals with the right real estate path, the results can be transformational.

## The Three Main Real Estate Investment Types

Let's break the field down into three broad categories:

Residential real estate – including single-family homes, townhouses, and small multifamily properties (two to four units) – is a common starting point for new investors due to its familiarity, easier financing, and lower entry costs, though it offers less scalability, greater vulnerability to vacancy, and fewer tax and leverage advantages compared to commercial real estate.

Commercial real estate – which includes office buildings, retail spaces, industrial properties, and hotels – offers higher income potential, longer lease terms, and financially stable corporate tenants, making it attractive for experienced investors seeking predictable cash flow and scale.

Multifamily real estate – defined as residential properties with five or more units – is classified as commercial by lenders and offers strong scalability, multiple income streams, and income-based financing, though it typically requires more capital, professional management, and faces stiff competition in high-demand markets.

## Why I Chose Multifamily

My early real estate career included both residential and commercial properties. I helped high-net-worth clients from around the world invest in New York City real estate – often in seven-figure office or apartment building deals. I also invested personally in residential homes, which gave me hands-on experience as a landlord.

But over time, I saw a pattern. Residential properties were easier to enter but harder to scale. Commercial office space was lucrative but subject to trends I couldn't always control.

Multifamily offered the best of both worlds: the tangibility and simplicity of residential real estate, combined with the income potential and scalability of commercial assets. But what truly set it apart was the sense of stability and control it offered. People will always need a place to live – and when a property is well-located and professionally managed, it doesn't just survive market shifts; it stays productive.

I saw this firsthand during the 2008 / 2009 real estate crash while advising a client who owned a seventy-two-unit property in Queens, NY. While other investments were collapsing, her building held firm. Occupancy stayed above 95 percent, rents remained consistent, and we even completed a value-add renovation that boosted NOI within a year. Watching that property weather the storm reinforced a powerful truth: with multifamily, you're not at the mercy of the market – you can take action, make decisions, and drive performance from the inside out.

That moment planted a seed. I realized I didn't just want to advise others on building wealth – I wanted to build it myself. It gave me the confidence and clarity to start investing, not just as a strategist, but as an owner. That experience became the foundation of my multifamily journey.

## Real Estate as a Wealth-Building Strategy

Whether you're starting with one small rental or scaling to more than 100 units, real estate offers several advantages:

- Cash flow: Recurring income that supports your lifestyle or gets reinvested.
- Appreciation: Long-term increase in value, especially in strong markets.
- Tax benefits: Depreciation, cost segregation, 1031 exchanges, and more.
- Leverage: Use other people's money (banks or partners) to grow your equity.
- Control: Unlike stocks, you can directly influence the value and performance of your investment.

Real estate is not a get-rich-quick game. It's a build-real-wealth-slowly-and-intentionally strategy, especially if you commit to learning the fundamentals, surrounding yourself with experts, and making informed, disciplined decisions.

## What This Book Will Help You Do

You don't need to be a financial expert or a real estate broker to succeed in real estate. But you do need to understand the field and choose your lane wisely. Beginning with Chapter 4, this book shifts from the foundational principles of multifamily real estate into the heart of what makes an investor truly successful: self-awareness, strategic action, and thoughtful execution. From this point forward, you'll not only learn what to do – but how to do it in a way that aligns with your goals, personality, and vision for the future. You'll define your unique investment identity, master deal analysis, build a high-performing team, and explore critical strategies around financing, operations, and scaling. Each chapter is designed to deepen your understanding and equip you with practical tools, real-world insights, and proven systems.

Before we crunch numbers or chase deals, we need to get crystal clear on one essential truth: real estate investing isn't one-size-fits-all. In Chapter 4, we turn the spotlight inward to help you uncover who you are as an investor – and why that matters more than any market metric. Your goals, your risk tolerance, your values, and your vision all shape the kind of portfolio you should build.

Anyone can find a property for sale. The real skill – and the real wealth – is in knowing how to separate a winning investment from an expensive mistake. In Chapter 5, we sharpen your deal-making instincts and give you the tools to evaluate opportunities with clarity and confidence.

In Chapter 6, you'll learn how to turn conversations into capital by mastering the subtle art of negotiation – one of the highest-return skills in your investor toolkit. Whether you're locking in a purchase price, structuring terms with a lender, or navigating contractor timelines, your words, tone, and strategy can dramatically shape the outcome. But this isn't about hardball tactics or intimidation – it's about connection, clarity, and creativity.

Forget the myth that you need deep pockets to get into multifamily real estate. What you really need is financial intelligence – the kind that allows you to leverage other people's money, manage risk like a pro, and unlock the capital you didn't even know you had access to. In Chapter 7, we pull back the curtain on the financing strategies that fuel serious growth.

In Chapter 8, Part 1, we take you behind the scenes of what it really takes to close a deal, not just find one. From scouting the right property to securing the right financing and aligning the right partners, the acquisition process is where vision meets execution.

This isn't just about checking boxes – it's about mastering the flow between deal, debt, and equity so each component supports the next. When you understand how these parts fit together, you don't just close deals – you close better deals. With less friction. Less risk. And a whole lot more upside. Whether it's your first acquisition or your fifteenth, this chapter offers a step-by-step road map to help you navigate the process like a seasoned pro and lay the groundwork for sustainable, scalable success.

Thus, in Chapter 8, Part 2, we dive into the art and science of raising equity for multifamily deals – not as a desperate plea for funds, but as an invitation for others to grow alongside you. Raising equity is about more than pitching a spreadsheet. It's about earning trust, communicating value, and showing potential investors – whether they're seasoned family offices, individual high-net-worth partners, or friends and colleagues – that your deal is worth their belief.

Behind every successful multifamily investor is a powerhouse team – the kind that turns good deals into great ones and great deals into scalable empires. In Chapter 9, we focus on how to build that team: not just with warm bodies, but with the right people in the right roles, aligned to your vision and values.

Real wealth isn't measured by gross income – it's measured by what stays in your pocket after taxes. In Chapter 10, we unlock one of the most underrated advantages of multifamily real estate: its ability to legally and strategically reduce your tax burden while growing your bottom line.

Every investment has its shadows – and in multifamily real estate, it's how you prepare for the unexpected that defines your success. In Chapter 11, we dive into the essential mindset and strategies behind effective risk management and problem-solving. Because protecting your investment isn't just about reacting to problems – it's about seeing them coming before they ever arrive.

In Chapter 12, we explore how to transform your property from a physical space into a living experience that resonates with tenants, investors, and the community. We dig into what it means to build a recognizable brand – one that communicates values, delivers a promise, and creates an emotional connection.

Acquiring a property is just the opening act. What truly determines your success is what comes next: how you manage, measure, and multiply the performance of that investment day after day. In Chapter 13, we shift the spotlight to operations – where real profit is earned and long-term wealth is built.

Eventually, every successful investor hits a milestone: the limit of their own capital. But far from being a setback, this moment signals growth. It's the point where your vision outpaces your wallet – and you're ready to bring others along for the ride. In Chapter 14, we dive into the essential skill of raising capital – not just as a fundraiser, but as a leader.

Every investor dreams of growing a portfolio that generates lasting wealth and impact. But moving from one property to many isn't just a numbers game – it's a leadership shift. In Chapter 15, we explore what it really takes to scale successfully, without sacrificing your sanity or your standards.

Multifamily real estate offers enormous potential – but with that potential comes responsibility. As an investor, you're not just managing properties; you're navigating a legal landscape that touches every aspect of ownership, operations, and tenant relationships.

In Chapter 16, we shine a light on the legal foundations every multifamily investor must understand to protect their assets, reputation, and peace of mind. From landlord-tenant laws and fair housing compliance to safety codes, lease structures, and liability issues, you'll learn how to spot legal landmines before they become costly mistakes.

Many investors begin in their own backyard – and for good reason. It's familiar, tangible, and within reach. But if you stop there, you risk missing the bigger picture. The most successful investors understand that the best opportunities often lie beyond their zip code. In Chapter 17, we break down how to confidently evaluate and invest in markets across the country – and even beyond.

In multifamily real estate, property management isn't just a support function – it's the heartbeat of your operation. Your management team is the face of your brand, the steward of your property, and the daily point of contact for your tenants. And what they do – or don't do – directly impacts your bottom line. In Chapter 18, we explore how to build a culture of excellence from the inside out.

When I transitioned from banking into real estate, I brought with me a deep respect for data, structure, and precision. In banking, decisions are guided by systems. In real estate, they often rely on instinct. I wanted to blend the two – and technology became the bridge. In Chapter 19, I share how leveraging digital tools, automation, and AI has transformed the way I invest, operate, and communicate.

In Chapter 20, we go beyond cash flow and equity to explore something deeper: how to turn your real estate journey into a generational story of purpose, prosperity, and impact. You'll learn how to involve your family in your investing vision, instill financial literacy and stewardship, and put the right systems in place to protect and grow what you've built.

As we close this book, I want to leave you with what I believe is the most powerful teacher in real estate – and in life: lived experience. And the best way to learn from it? Through stories. Throughout my multifamily journey, I've encountered wins, setbacks, near misses, and breakthroughs. In this chapter, I share real client stories and case studies that bring the principles of this book to life – not in theory, but in practice.

A great multifamily investor knows that the exit is just as important as the entry. In fact, your returns are often determined not by what you bought, but by how – and when – you chose to move on. In Chapter 22, we dive into one of the most strategic (and overlooked) aspects of real estate investing: knowing how to exit with intention and optimize your portfolio for long-term growth.

In Chapter 23, we bring it all together. This isn't just a recap – it's your launchpad. Whether you're preparing for your first deal or ready to scale into new markets, this chapter offers a practical, personalized road map to help you move forward with clarity and momentum.

You now have a bird's-eye view of the journey ahead – one filled with insight, practical tools, and tested strategies that will equip you to become a confident, capable multifamily investor. Whether you're transitioning from single-family properties like I once did or starting fresh with a bold vision for the future, this book is your guide. Keep turning the pages, stay open to new ideas, and let each chapter move you closer to building the wealth, freedom, and impact you desire.

## Key Areas to Know in Multifamily Real Estate

## Investing.

Market research involves analyzing economic indicators, multifamily supply and demand trends, vacancy rates, rent growth, and identifying emerging neighborhoods to make informed, data-driven investment decisions.

Competitive analysis involves evaluating comparable properties, amenities, pricing, tenant demographics, and market dynamics – including absorption rates and upcoming construction – to assess positioning and identify opportunities to outperform the competition.

Regulatory environment refers to the legal framework governing zoning, land use, landlord-tenant laws, rent control, and tax policies, all of which can significantly impact the feasibility, profitability, and risk of a multifamily investment.

Economic and demographic trends encompass migration patterns, population shifts, key renter demographics, and infrastructure developments – all of which influence rental demand, market stability, and long-term investment potential in multifamily real estate.

Risk assessment involves identifying potential market, economic, political, and environmental threats – such as oversupply, downturns, interest rate fluctuations, and local policy shifts – to proactively manage and mitigate the impact on your multifamily investment.

Networking and information sources are essential for success in multifamily investing, involving active participation in real estate associations, leveraging industry publications and data services, and building strong relationships with brokers, property managers, and fellow investors to stay informed and uncover opportunities.

## Conclusion

Mastering the real estate landscape is about more than knowing property types – it's about understanding the economic forces, market dynamics, regulatory environment, and competitive context that shape every investment decision. Whether you're analyzing trends, assessing risks, or building strategic relationships, this foundational knowledge gives you the confidence to move forward with clarity and purpose. The most successful multifamily investors don't just react to the market – they read it, anticipate it, and position themselves ahead of the curve.

## Reflection Questions

1. What drew you to real estate investing in the first place?
2. Reflect on whether it was income, wealth-building, autonomy, or something else.
3. Which real estate asset class appeals to you the most right now – residential, commercial, or multifamily – and why?
4. Consider your current lifestyle, capital, experience, and risk tolerance.
5. Have you ever lived in or owned a property that could be classified as an investment property? What did you learn from that experience?
6. How comfortable are you with managing properties and tenants directly? Would you prefer to be hands-on or hire a management company?
7. What concerns do you have about real estate investing – and how might you begin addressing them?
8. (e.g., financing, property management, market risk, lack of experience)
9. What do you want your real estate portfolio to help you accomplish in the next five to ten years?
10. Write out specific personal or financial goals.
11. Are there markets or property types you're curious about but haven't explored yet? What's holding you back?

# CHAPTER 4:
# FINDING YOUR
# INVESTMENT IDENTITY

*"Knowing yourself is the beginning of all wisdom."*
— Aristotle

Before we dive into numbers, spreadsheets, and financial modeling, let's start with something even more critical: identity.

The sun was just starting to rise as he turned the key and pushed open the rusted gate to Building C. The faint smell of fresh paint battled with the more familiar scent of old carpet and long-forgotten furniture. It was quiet – too quiet – but in that silence was a sense of promise.

This was it. His first multifamily purchase. Twenty-four units of potential, problems, and possibility.

He stood still for a moment in the gravel lot, a clipboard in one hand, his phone buzzing in the other. The bank had wired the funds at 4:57 p.m. the day before – just in time. The seller's agent had already moved on to the next deal. And here he was now, the new owner. No turning back.

But what exactly had he bought?

Yes, a building. Yes, cash flow. Yes, deferred maintenance and a long list of upgrades.

But more than that – he had bought into a vision.

The real question wasn't *what* he bought. It was *who* he was becoming.

You see, before the spreadsheets and the due diligence reports, before the cap rates and the rent rolls, there's something deeper that must be uncovered – your investment identity. The lens through which you see opportunities. The filter that guides your decision-making. The foundation for every risk you will or won't take.

This chapter is about finding that identity – because no two investors are the same, and neither are their paths to success. Some buy for legacy, others for lifestyle. Some crave control, while others thrive in partnerships. What drives you? What do you want your money to do for you – and why?

Let's explore the moment *before* the deal – the clarity of purpose that will determine everything that follows.

Let me introduce you to Joseph. He was an enthusiastic, hardworking amateur investor with big dreams. Like many others, he believed real estate was the path to financial freedom – and he was right about that. But where Joseph went wrong was how he began.

Joseph skipped the self-discovery step. He didn't take the time to identify his goals, understand his risk tolerance, or evaluate how much time and energy he could – or wanted to – commit to managing a property. He had no clear strategy, no investment criteria, no road map.

## Self-Discovery: What Joseph Didn't Know about Himself

Joseph thought he was ready. He had the down payment, a mentor on speed dial, and a spreadsheet that showed the building would cash flow from day one.

But within six months, the cracks started to show – not just in the foundation of the property, but in his own mindset.

He found himself second-guessing decisions, feeling overwhelmed by late-night calls from tenants, hesitating when it came time to raise rents or hire help. He wasn't sleeping. His confidence waned. For all the financial projections he had modeled, he had missed one critical variable: himself.

Joseph hadn't asked the hard questions – the ones that get to the heart of investment identity.

Here are the questions he should have asked before buying that property:

- What kind of investor am I?
- Do I want to be hands-on, or do I thrive when I delegate? Do I want to build an empire, or secure a few solid assets for long-term wealth?
- What's my true tolerance for risk and uncertainty?
- Can I stomach vacancy dips, emergency repairs, and slow leasing seasons – or do I need stability and predictability to sleep at night?
- Why am I doing this – really?
- Is it for financial freedom, generational wealth, control over my time, or proving something to myself or others?
- How do I handle stress and decision-making under pressure?
- When things go sideways (and they will), do I lean in or shut down?
- What does success look like for me – in five years, in ten?
- Am I chasing a number, a lifestyle, a legacy, or an impact?
- What am I unwilling to sacrifice?
- Time with family? My health? My sense of peace?

Joseph hadn't taken the time to define his answers, and as a result, the property began to define him. It shaped his days, his emotions, his confidence – because he entered the deal without anchoring his decisions in identity.

Multifamily investing is not one size-fits-all. Before you build a portfolio, build a mirror. Know who you are, what you want, and how you work. Otherwise, you'll find your-self owning something that owns you.

When Joseph found a multifamily property in a Class A location but a Class C asset, he jumped at the chance. On the surface, it looked like a great investment. Prime zip code, nice neighborhood, strong rental demand. But there was one critical problem: the building was constructed in 1965 and required a high level of ongoing maintenance. Class C properties are older, often built before the 1980s, and may require significant renovations.

Joseph had overpaid. He didn't properly assess the condition of the property or calculate how much the re-pairs and upkeep would cost him. As expenses piled up and his expected cash flow disappeared, regret set in. He felt stuck, frustrated, and overwhelmed – all because he skipped the first step: defining who he was as an investor and what kind of investments aligned with that identity. Joseph's story is a cautionary tale. It's a reminder that the first and most important step in multifamily investing is understanding yourself.

In this chapter, we'll walk through a process of self-discovery. You'll clarify your investment goals, determine your level of involvement, assess your available resources, and uncover your "why." Are you building for income, appreciation, time freedom, legacy – or a mix of all four?

When you understand who you are as an investor, you'll stop chasing deals that don't align with your vision. You'll gain clarity, reduce risk, and move forward with the confidence of someone who knows exactly what they're building – and why.

Let Joseph's early mistake be your lesson. This chapter will help you get clear, stay focused, and begin investing with intention.

Real estate success isn't just about what you invest in – it's about *who* you are as an investor. Without a clear identi-ty, it's easy to fall into decision fatigue, chase every shiny object, or follow someone else's strategy that doesn't fit your life or goals. But when you take the time to define your investment identity, your purpose, your preferences, your risk tolerance – you create a personal blueprint for sustainable growth.

Some investors thrive on flipping distressed homes for quick profit. Others prefer steady, long-term cash flow from well-managed apartment buildings. Some build portfolios full-time, while others invest passively to supplement their careers or retirement.

Before you start buying properties or raising capital, you need to define one thing clearly: Who are you as an investor?

This chapter will help you answer those questions so you can avoid chasing trends and instead create a real estate strategy that works for your goals, your resources, and your life.

## Why Identity Matters

Successful real estate investing starts with knowing your strategy in alignment with your goals, risk tolerance, time, capital, preferred level of involvement, and long-term vision. Following someone else's path without that personal clarity often leads to costly missteps and burnout.

Clarify your Goals by asking why you're investing in real estate – whether for cash flow, long-term wealth, diversification, income replacement, or legacy – because your strategy must directly align with your purpose to produce meaningful and sustainable results.

Know Your Risk Tolerance by honestly assessing your comfort with volatility, debt, and market fluctuations – so you can choose investments, whether stabilized or value-add, that match your financial resilience and peace of mind. Every investment comes with some risk – vacancy, market shifts, repairs, or even bad tenants. You need to assess how much volatility you're willing to accept.

Assess Your Resources by evaluating your available time, capital, and skills – so you can build a realistic strategy, identify where you may need partners, and play to your strengths without overextending yourself. If you're light on one area, you can often compensate by partnering with others. But knowing your strengths and limits is key.

Active versus Passive Investing is about choosing your level of involvement – whether you want to be hands-on managing deals and operations or hands-off providing capital and earning returns – so you can align your real estate journey with your lifestyle, experience, and long-term goals. Many investors start active to learn the ropes, then shift to passive for scale and lifestyle freedom. Others build a hybrid model.

## Define Your Buy Box

Set clear criteria for the type of multifamily properties you seek – such as location, size, price range, and asset class – so you can stay focused, avoid distractions, and ensure every opportunity aligns with your strategy and investment identity.

For example, if you've decided to invest in twenty- to fifty-unit properties in secondary markets with strong job growth, don't let a shiny listing for a luxury duplex in a trendy urban core pull you off track. It might be a great deal for someone else – but if it doesn't fit *your* buy box, it's a distraction, not an opportunity.

One of the best tools you can use to stay focused as an investor is your "buy box." Your buy box is a clearly defined set of criteria that outlines the type of multifamily properties you're actively looking to acquire. It helps filter out distractions and keeps you aligned with your goals.

## Here's My Buy Box

Location: Secondary or tertiary markets in Florida with job growth and population increases (e.g., West Palm Beach, Fort Lauderdale, Miami suburbs)

- Property Type: Multifamily only, garden-style preferred
- Class: Class B or C properties in Class B neighborhoods

- Units: 100 to 200 units
- Year Built: Nineties or newer, with updated electrical and plumbing preferred
- Target Cap Rate: Minimum of 6 percent at acquisition
- Value-Add Potential: Light to moderate rehab (interior upgrades, deferred maintenance, improved management)
- Price Range: $30 to 60 million
- Ownership Structure: Joint venture or syndication, open to bringing in co-GPs
- Hold Period: Five to seven years with value-add repositioning and refinance at year four, subject to interest rates.

Defining your buy box helps streamline your deal flow, improve your underwriting discipline, and communicate clearly with brokers, partners, and investors. It evolves as you grow, but even a first version gives you the clarity to act with intention and avoid costly missteps – like the one Joseph made.

## My Own Investment Identity

My identity as an investor evolved over time. In the beginning, I was an advisor – helping high-net-worth clients diversify their holdings. As I began investing personally, I realized I was drawn to multifamily properties that needed vision and strategic improvement.

I'm a hands-on strategist – I enjoy seeing the numbers, walking the property, building the team, and optimizing performance. But I also value balance, so I work with property managers and partners to scale sustainably.

**Why?** Because for me, it's not just about transactions – it's about transformation.

I find deep satisfaction in taking something underperforming and bringing it to life. I enjoy the numbers because they tell a story – one that I can shape. Walking the property gives me a tangible connection to the asset. Building the team means I'm creating opportunity and alignment. And optimizing performance isn't just about profit – it's about excellence, pride, and purpose.

At the core, I enjoy being a hands-on strategist because it allows me to combine vision with action. It gives me agency. But I also know that success isn't sustainable if it costs me my health, peace, or time with loved ones – which is why I've learned to balance control with trust, ambition with delegation.

That's the real strategy – knowing when to hold on and when to let go.

My goal is not just wealth – but freedom, impact, and legacy.

## Your Identity Is Allowed to Evolve

You don't have to get it all right today. Your identity will shift as you grow, learn, and succeed. The key is to start from a place of clarity and intention, rather than blindly following the crowd.

In the next chapter, we'll take this identity and put it to work as we explore how to source and evaluate real estate deals – so you can begin turning strategy into action.

## Conclusion

Clarity is power. When you know who you are as an investor, what drives you, what you value, and how you want to engage – you begin to filter opportunities through intention rather than impulse. You stop comparing yourself to others and start building a strategy that reflects your unique life and goals. In the next chapter, we'll take that identity and put it into action by showing you how to source and evaluate real estate deals that fit your vision – and move you one step closer to the portfolio and future you're meant to create.

## Finding Your Investment Identity Checklist

*Self-Assessment*

- Define your personal financial goals (income, wealth building, legacy).
- Assess your risk tolerance and investment time horizon.
- Identify your strengths and areas for development in real estate investing.

### *Investment Style Exploration*

- Research different multifamily investment approaches (value-add, core, opportunistic).
- Determine which property types and markets align with your preferences.
- Consider your desired level of involvement (hands-on versus passive).

### *Goal Alignment*

- Align investment choices with your lifestyle, family commitments, and time availability.
- Establish measurable milestones and success criteria.
- Set expectations for returns, cash flow, and portfolio growth.

### *Resource Evaluation*

- Inventory your financial resources, credit availability, and capital partners.
- Identify your network and support team for investing activities.

### *Learning and Growth Plan*

- Commit to ongoing education in areas where you need improvement.
- Seek mentorship or coaching tailored to your investment goals.

### *Strategic Planning*

- Develop an investment mission statement or guiding principles.

- Draft an initial investment plan incorporating your identity and goals.
- Schedule regular reviews to refine and adjust your investment identity as you gain experience.

**Reflection Questions**
1. What are your top three reasons for wanting to invest in real estate?
2. (e.g., passive income, wealth-building, legacy, tax benefits, financial freedom)
3. What does success in real estate look like for you five years from now?
4. Be specific; how many properties, how much monthly cash flow, what kind of lifestyle?
5. How would you describe your risk tolerance?
6. Are you more comfortable with stable, low-risk returns – or are you open to higher risk for higher potential gain?
7. How much time can you realistically dedicate to real estate investing each week or month?
8. Based on your current schedule, are you better suited for an active or passive investing role?
9. What financial resources do you have available to begin or grow your portfolio?
10. Think about your personal capital, potential partner funds, and borrowing capacity.
11. What unique strengths or experiences do you bring to real estate investing?
12. (e.g., finance background, project management, negotiation skills, deal analysis)
13. What aspects of investing do you feel least confident about right now?
14. Make a list of topics you'd like to learn more about or skills you'd like to develop.
15. Describe your ideal investment property.
16. (Location, size, condition, tenant profile, target return, etc.)
17. Who could you partner with to complement

your strengths and fill your gaps?
18. Think of mentors, professionals, or potential joint venture partners.
19. What would a real estate investment strategy that aligns with your life and values look like?
20. Be honest – how does it support your family, career, health, and freedom goals?

# CHAPTER 5:
# SOURCING AND ANALYZING DEAL

*"An investment in knowledge pays the best interest."*
— Benjamin Franklin

Finding a multifamily deal is one thing. Knowing whether it's a good deal – or a bad one in disguise – is something else entirely.

## Let Me Tell You About Arturo

Arturo stared at the maintenance report in disbelief. The roof that was supposed to have "five good years left" was actively leaking into three units. The HVAC system had failed in the middle of a summer heat wave. And the "strong future rents" the seller promised? They were pure fiction – local comps were nowhere near the pro forma numbers.

Tenants were upset. Repairs were piling up. And the property manager was calling daily with new problems. This was not the investment Arturo had envisioned.

So how did he get here?

Just six months earlier, Arturo was full of energy, ambition, and spreadsheets. He was smart, motivated, and determined to break into the multifamily game. Like many new investors, he had spent countless hours scouring online platforms, chasing what looked like "deals."

Then it appeared: a listing in a fast-growing market, polished with attractive photos and a promising projected return. The seller's brochure painted a rosy picture – strong future rents, low expenses, upward-trending market growth. It looked too good to pass up, so Arturo didn't.

He didn't walk the property. He didn't verify the comps. He didn't have a clearly defined buy box – just a desire to own something fast and a belief that multifamily was the golden ticket. He mistook urgency for opportunity.

What Arturo lacked wasn't intelligence – it was alignment. He hadn't clarified his investment identity, his real goals, or his non-negotiables. He was following someone else's playbook, not his own.

Arturo's story is a cautionary tale, but also a common one. The path to successful investing doesn't start with a deal – it starts with you.

But Arturo made a critical mistake. He didn't dig into the actual numbers – the trailing twelve months (T12) of financial performance that tell the real story of a property. Instead of verifying actual rent rolls, repair costs, occupancy data, and operating expenses, he relied on the seller's pro forma projections.

Reality hit hard.

The building had higher vacancy than listed, repairs were constant and underbudgeted, and the rents were inflated compared to actual collections. Arturo's "deal" quickly turned into a lemon. What should have been a steady cash-flowing investment became a financial and emotional drain.

Arturo's story is a powerful reminder: If you don't verify the numbers, you're gambling. And most gamblers lose.

No matter how good a property looks on paper – or online – your ability to analyze the real numbers is what separates success from regret.

In this chapter, we'll walk through how to source deals wisely and how to analyze them with clarity, discipline, and confidence. We'll cover what to look for in financial statements, how to compare pro forma versus actuals, how to spot red flags, and how to stress-test assumptions.

You've defined who you are as an investor. Now it's time to find the deals that align with your strategy – and evaluate them like a professional.

The good news? Great deals are out there. The challenge is that they rarely scream "great deal" on the surface. They hide behind outdated listings, cosmetic damage, tough tenants, or complex financials. To find them, you'll need a combination of networking, tools, and discipline.

And once you find them, you'll need to know exactly what to look for to determine if it's worth your time and capital.

## Where to Find Investment Deals

MLS and Public Listings is where real estate agents post properties for sale. While often saturated with retail-priced deals, the MLS can yield opportunities if you move quickly or focus on overlooked listings.

## Off-Market Deals

Off-market deals are properties that aren't publicly listed and are typically sourced through direct outreach, personal networks, or referrals. Because they aren't on the open market, they often come with less competition, more room to negotiate, and greater flexibility in structuring the terms.

For example, I once contacted a multifamily property owner directly and simply asked if he'd be open to selling. He hadn't listed the property, but he was willing to talk. We negotiated a fair price, and I structured the deal to meet his needs – including a flexible closing timeline and a short-term leaseback – which made the transaction a win for both of us.

Commercial Platforms are sites like LoopNet, Crexi, and PropertyShark that list multifamily and commercial properties. These are great for early deal research and broker outreach.

Local Meetups and Investor Groups offer valuable opportunities to build relationships with investors and brokers, often leading to early access to deals, strategic partnerships, and potential passive investment opportunities.

## How to Evaluate a Deal

Sourcing deals is only half the battle. Knowing how to run the numbers is where good investors become great ones.

Here are the key metrics and what they mean:

### *Net Operating Income (NOI)*

NOI = Gross Rental Income – Operating Expenses. This is the property's true income before debt service. It helps you measure performance and value. NOI helps investors and lenders assess the true profitability of a property's operations and is central to valuing income-producing real estate.

### *Cap Rate (Capitalization Rate)*

Cap Rate = NOI ÷ Purchase Price. Cap rate tells you about the return on a property if you paid all cash. It varies by market. A higher cap rate usually means higher risk. Cap rate, for example, is a great metric when you're comparing properties in different markets or gauging whether a deal is fairly priced based on net operating income (NOI). But if you're trying to figure out how much your personal investment is earning you, especially if you're using leverage, then cash-on-cash return is your go-to number. It's the investor's lens for understanding short-term yield.

### *Cash-on-Cash Return*

Cash-on-cash return is one of the most practical metrics in real estate investing. It tells you how much cash you're getting back each year compared to how much cash you put in.

The formula is simple:

Cash-on-Cash = Annual Cash Flow ÷ Initial Cash Invested

But the insight it gives you? That's powerful.

"This is the number I always ask first," one seasoned investor told me. "If I'm putting in $100,000, how fast is that money coming back to me?"

Cash-on-cash is especially important when you're using leverage – because it focuses on your actual out-of-pocket investment, not the full value of the property. It cuts through the noise of appreciation forecasts and tax benefits and shows you what really matters: How much cash is hitting your account every year.

If you're investing for passive income, this metric keeps you grounded. It answers the essential question: Is this deal delivering real returns today – not just on paper, but in practice?

### *Debt Service Coverage Ratio (DSCR)*

DSCR = NOI ÷ Annual Debt Payments. Lenders look for a DSCR of at least 1.20 to 1.25. A ratio below 1.0 means the property doesn't generate enough to cover the loan.

Debt Service Coverage Ratio (DSCR) is one of the key metrics lenders use to evaluate the risk of financing a multifamily property. It measures a property's ability to cover its debt obligations using its Net Operating Income (NOI). The formula is simple: DSCR = NOI ÷ Annual Debt Payments. A DSCR of 1.0 means the property brings in just enough income to pay its debt – no cushion, no margin for error. Most lenders look for a DSCR of at least 1.20 to 1.25, which signals that the property generates 20 to 25 percent more income than it needs to meet its loan payments. A DSCR below 1.0 is a red flag – it means the property is losing money and will require out-of-pocket support from the investor. As a borrower, understanding your DSCR not only helps you qualify for financing but also gives you a clear picture of how financially resilient your investment really is.

### *Internal Rate of Return (IRR)*

IRR reflects your total return over time, including appreciation. It's useful for long-term or value-add deals but more complex to calculate. IRR is your best tool for analyzing long-term value creation over time – it factors in your entire investment horizon, including exit strategies and timing. And when it comes to the bank's perspective, DSCR tells you whether the property generates enough income to cover its debt. It's a lender's way of asking, "Will this deal pay for itself with room to spare?"

Red flags to watch for include underestimated expenses, inflated rent projections, deferred maintenance, and low debt service coverage ratios – all of which can significantly impact a property's true performance and should be carefully vetted before moving forward.

## Example: A Quick Deal Snapshot

Let's say you find a ten-unit multifamily building listed for $1.2 million.

- Gross Income: $120,000 per year
- Operating Expenses: $45,000 per year
- NOI: $75,000
- Cap Rate = $75,000 ÷ $1,200,000 = 6.25 percent

If you put $300,000 down and finance the rest:

- Annual Debt Payments = $40,000
- Cash Flow = $75,000 – $40,000 = $35,000
- Cash-on-Cash Return = $35,000 ÷ $300,000 = 11.67 percent

This would be considered a solid deal, assuming condition, location, and rent comps support the numbers.

By the end of this chapter, you won't just recognize these terms – you'll know how to apply them strategically, depending on your goals, your risk tolerance, and the deal in front of you. Because great investing isn't about finding every deal – it's about recognizing the right one and walking away from the rest.

## The Importance of Discipline

Smart investors don't chase every shiny object. They run the numbers, stick to their buy box, and walk away when deals don't meet their criteria. Some of the best deals I've ever made were the ones I didn't do – because the numbers didn't justify the risk.

Stick to your identity, trust your math, and stay aligned with your long-term vision.

Finding and analyzing multifamily deals is part art, part science. The more you practice, the more refined your instincts become – and the easier it is to separate solid opportunities from costly distractions.

Discipline is your edge. Let your investment criteria guide you. If a deal doesn't fit, walk away – no matter how tempting it looks on the surface. Stay focused on the properties that align with your goals, strategy, and identity.

With patience and persistence, the right opportunities will appear – and when they do, you'll be ready to act with clarity and confidence, building the portfolio you've envisioned from the start.

## Conclusion

Sourcing and analyzing deals is where preparation meets opportunity. The best investors don't just wait for the perfect property to fall into their lap – they build systems, relationships, and habits that consistently surface quality opportunities. By defining your buy box, mastering the numbers, watching for red flags, and staying disciplined in your underwriting, you move from reactive to strategic. Remember, a great deal isn't just found – it's recognized. And the more deals you analyze, the sharper your instincts will become. With the right approach, you won't just find deals – you'll find the right ones.

## Sourcing and Analyzing Deals Checklist

### Deal Sourcing

- Build a network of brokers, property managers,

and wholesalers.

- Leverage online platforms and MLS for deal opportunities.
- Attend local real estate networking events and auctions.
- Develop relationships with property owners for off-market deals.

### Initial Deal Screening

- Verify that the property location aligns with your investment criteria.
- Review basic property information: size, units, occupancy, and condition.
- Assess the asking price relative to market comparables.

### Comprehensive Due Diligence

- Obtain and analyze rent rolls and lease agreements.
- Review financial statements, operating expenses, and capital expenditure history.
- Conduct property inspections or hire qualified inspectors.
- Evaluate the physical condition and identify deferred maintenance needs.
- Investigate zoning, code compliance, and legal issues.

### Market Analysis

- Assess neighborhood trends, demographics, and local economic indicators.
- Research comparable rental rates and vacancy rates.
- Evaluate future development plans and potential risks in the area.

### *Financial Modeling and Underwriting*

- Create detailed cash flow projections based on realistic assumptions.
- Calculate key metrics: NOI, cap rate, cash-on-cash return, IRR.
- Stress-test scenarios for vacancy, rent growth, and expenses.
- Compare the deal to alternative investment opportunities.

### *Decision-Making*

- Identify deal strengths, weaknesses, opportunities, and threats (SWOT analysis).
- Determine fit with your investment strategy and risk tolerance.
- Plan a negotiation strategy based on analysis.

## Reflection Questions

1. Where will you begin your deal search?
2. (MLS, off-market outreach, commercial platforms, networking?) What steps can you take this week to begin sourcing?
3. What relationships do you need to build to access better deals?
4. (e.g., brokers, property managers, wholesalers, lenders)
5. What is your acquisition criteria?
6. Define your ideal investment criteria in terms of:
   - Location
   - Property type and size
   - Price range
   - Target cap rate or cash-on-cash return
   - Risk level
7. Do you feel confident analyzing deals on your own?
8. If not, what tools, resources, or training do you

need to sharpen your analysis skills?

9. What deal evaluation metrics are most important to you – and why? (e.g., Cash-on-Cash Return, Cap Rate, DSCR, IRR)

10. How much risk are you willing to take in a deal that has strong upside potential but needs significant renovation or repositioning?

11. What red flags will be non-negotiable deal-breakers for you?

12. List the financial or physical conditions that would cause you to walk away.

13. Have you built a basic underwriting spreadsheet or acquired one?

14. If not, will you create one or find a template you can start with?

15. How many deals are you committed to analyzing each week? (Set a target to build your skill and increase your chances of finding the right property.)

16. What will success look like for you in the next ninety days?

17. Will it be touring your first property, making your first offer, or locking in your first deal?

# CHAPTER 6:
# NEGOTIATION SKILLS FOR REAL ESTATE INVESTORS – MASTERING THE ART TO MAXIMIZE VALUE

*"Negotiation is not about winning a battle; it's about creating a solution where all parties feel they've gained value."*

— Anonymous

You don't get rich by spotting a deal. You get rich by negotiating it well. Whether you're discussing price with a seller, terms with a lender, commission with a broker, or timelines with a contractor, your ability to negotiate effectively can significantly impact your profitability and success. Good negotiation isn't about being aggressive or confrontational; it's about building rapport, understanding interests, and finding mutually beneficial solutions that keep deals moving forward.

This chapter explores how to develop negotiation skills tailored for real estate investing, with practical techniques to improve deal terms and project outcomes.

Understand the interests behind positions by uncovering each party's true motivations – whether it's a seller's need for speed, a broker's focus on closing, a lender's risk concerns, or a contractor's workflow. By knowing why each party wants what they want, you can tailor your approach to address their core concerns while advancing your goals and moving the deal forward effectively.

**Preparation is key.** Knowing the numbers, setting clear objectives, anticipating objections, and practicing your pitch equips you with the confidence and credibility needed to negotiate effectively and seize the right opportunities. Preparation builds confidence and positions you as a serious, credible negotiator.

I remember one deal where preparation made all the difference. I was negotiating with a seller who wanted top dollar for a property with significant deferred maintenance. Because I had already walked the property, reviewed repair estimates, and pulled comps from the surrounding neighborhood, I was able to calmly present a counteroffer – backed by data – that reflected the true condition and value of the asset. The seller initially resisted, but the clarity of my numbers and logic shifted the conversation. We closed the deal $80,000 below asking.

Contrast that with an earlier experience where I walked into a negotiation without doing my homework. I hadn't reviewed the rent roll in detail or verified the expenses. When the seller pushed back on price, I didn't have a strong footing – and I lost the deal to a more prepared buyer. That lesson stuck.

In multifamily real estate, the best negotiators aren't always the loudest – they're the most prepared.

## Build Rapport and Establish

**Trust** by approaching negotiations with respect, empathy, and transparency – because people are far more likely to work with and offer favorable terms to those they genuinely trust and connect with. People prefer to do business with those they trust, so investing in rapport can pay dividends in better terms and smoother deals.

## Use Tactical Concessions

Offer low-cost, high-value trade-offs *strategically and conditionally*. Every give should be tied to a get. This keeps you in control and builds momentum without giving away leverage. Track every concession – small trades can add up fast.

## Communicate Clearly and Confidently

Use concise language, a calm tone, and positive framing – while asking open-ended questions – to foster trust, avoid misunderstandings, and strengthen your position in any negotiation. Effective communication helps avoid misunderstandings and builds credibility. Maintain a calm and composed tone, even under pressure. Ask open-ended questions to encourage dialogue and reveal more information.

## Leverage Data and Facts

Do this by using comps, cost estimates, and financial projections to justify your position – turning negotiations into objective, solutions-focused discussions that build credibility and minimize emotional bias. Numbers and data are powerful tools in negotiation. Data-driven negotiation reduces emotional bias and builds a logical case.

## Know When to Walk Away

The best deals come after a 'no.' If the terms don't work, let it go. Then wait for the follow-up call. Walking away can be the most powerful move in securing better opportunities ahead. A strong negotiator knows their limits and when to exit. Sometimes, walking away opens opportunities to revisit the deal on better terms later.

## Negotiating with Specific Parties

This means tailoring your approach – highlighting speed and certainty with sellers, setting clear expectations with brokers, leveraging offers with lenders, and defining scope and accountability with contractors – to build trust while securing favorable terms across the board. Sellers: Emphasize your preparedness, financing strength, and ability to close quickly. Be patient but firm on price and contingencies.

Brokers: Respect their role but negotiate commission if justified by deal size or if working exclusively. Clarify expectations upfront. Lenders: Negotiate rates, fees, and terms by shopping around and leveraging multiple offers. Understand their risk assessment criteria. Contractors: Clarify the scope of work, timelines, and payment terms upfront. Negotiate guarantees or penalties for delays or quality issues.

## *Example*

While negotiating the purchase of a fifty-unit apartment complex, I discovered the seller was motivated by an urgent relocation. By offering a flexible closing timeline and a short due diligence period, I was able to negotiate a $250,000 reduction off the asking price while still accommodating the seller's needs. Additionally, by requesting a detailed scope from the contractor and tying payments to milestones, I kept renovation costs under control, preserving project profitability.

Negotiation is a skill that can be learned and refined over time. By understanding motivations, preparing thoroughly, communicating effectively, and knowing your limits, you can consistently negotiate better deals and improve your project outcomes. The art of negotiation is less about winning every battle and more about building lasting relationships and creating value for all parties involved.

## Negotiation Skills Checklist for Real Estate Investors

### *Preparation*

Prepare thoroughly by researching the property, defining clear objectives, anticipating objections, and practicing your pitch to enter negotiations with confidence, clarity, and control.

### *Building Rapport*

Involves approaching all parties with respect, listening to understand their motivations, finding common ground, and being honest and transparent to establish trust and foster collaborative negotiations.

## Negotiation Tactics

*Use data and facts to support your offers and counteroffers.*

**Example**: When negotiating the purchase price of an apartment building, I always show the seller's real estate broker recent sales data of comparable properties in the neighborhood showing lower prices per unit. This objective market data supports my offer and justifies why my offer is fair.

*Offer low-cost concessions with high perceived value strategically.*

**Example**: To persuade a seller to accept a lower price, I often offer a flexible closing date that aligns with the seller's relocation plans. This accommodation costs me little but may be valuable to the seller, making my offer more attractive.

*Request reciprocal concessions when you give something.*

*Example:* Depending on the acquisition, sometimes I agree to waive a minor inspection contingency to speed up the deal but ask the seller to cover some of the closing costs in return. This ensures I don't give up value without receiving something beneficial.

*Communicate clearly, calmly, and confidently.*

**Example**: During a tense price discussion, I calmly explain my rationale, highlighting market data and my investment criteria without raising my voice or becoming defensive. Clear and composed communication helps keep negotiations productive.

*Ask open-ended questions to encourage dialogue and uncover information.*

*Example:* Instead of asking, "Will you lower the price?" I always ask, "What factors are most important in this sale?" This invites the seller to share his priorities, revealing opportunities to tailor my offer to meet his needs.

## Conclusion

Great real estate investors aren't just deal finders – they're skilled negotiators who know how to turn opportunity into advantage. Whether you're working with sellers, brokers, lenders, or contractors, your ability to prepare, build rapport, communicate clearly, and leverage data directly impacts your success. **Aim for a win-win negotiation – one that meets your goals and keeps the relationship strong enough to do business again.**

With the right mindset and strategies, you can secure better terms, protect your downside, and build a portfolio that reflects both financial strength and professional integrity.

## Negotiation Skills Checklist for Real Estate Investors

### *Preparation*

- Research property details thoroughly, including market comps and repair costs.
- Define your negotiation goals: target price, must-haves, and deal breakers.
- Anticipate possible objections and prepare responses.
- Practice your negotiation pitch and key talking points.

### *Building Rapport*

- Approach negotiations with respect and professionalism.
- Listen actively to understand the other party's motivations and concerns.
- Find common ground to create collaborative solutions.
- Be honest and transparent where appropriate.

### *Negotiation Techniques*

- Use data and factual evidence to support your

offers.

- Offer low-cost, high-value concessions strategically.
- Request reciprocal concessions when making compromises.
- Communicate clearly, calmly, and confidently.
- Ask open-ended questions to uncover deeper insights.

### Dealing with Specific Parties

- Tailor negotiation approaches for sellers, brokers, lenders, and contractors.
- Highlight your strengths (e.g., financing readiness) with sellers.
- Negotiate broker commissions fairly based on deal complexity.
- Shop around and negotiate loan terms with lenders.
- Clarify scope, timelines, and payment terms upfront with contractors.

### Knowing When to Walk Away

- Establish your maximum price and minimum acceptable terms before negotiating.
- Recognize red flags and deal-breakers early.
- Be prepared to pause or exit negotiations if terms are unfavorable.

### Post-Negotiation

- Document agreed terms clearly in writing.
- Maintain professionalism to preserve relationships for future dealings.

## Reflection Questions

1. How do you currently prepare for negotiations with sellers, brokers, lenders, and contractors?
2. What steps can you take to improve your prepa-

ration process?

3. How well do you understand the interests and motivations of the other parties in your deals?
4. How might better understanding these help you negotiate more effectively?
5. What strategies do you use to build rapport and trust during negotiations?
6. Can you identify opportunities to strengthen your relationships with key stakeholders?
7. Are you comfortable making and receiving concessions in negotiations?
8. How can you use concessions more strategically to create win-win outcomes?
9. How do you ensure clear and confident communication during negotiations?
10. What communication habits could you develop or improve?
11. Do you use data and facts to support your negotiating positions?
12. How might better use of market information influence your deals?
13. Have you identified your deal-breakers and limits before entering negotiations?
14. Are you comfortable walking away when terms don't meet your criteria?
15. How do you tailor your negotiation style when dealing with different parties (sellers, brokers, lenders, contractors)?
16. What has been your biggest negotiation challenge in real estate investing, and what did you learn from it?
17. What is one specific negotiation skill or technique you want to focus on developing next?

# CHAPTER 7:
# FINANCING STRATEGIES FOR MULTIFAMILY REAL ESTATE

*"It's not your money that builds wealth
– it's what you do with it."*

— Robert Kiyosaki

You don't need millions in the bank. You need to understand how money works.

Financing is one of the most powerful tools in real estate investing, and when used wisely, it allows you to scale faster, reduce risk, and control high-value assets with a fraction of the capital.

In Chapter 7, we'll explore the many ways to fund your multifamily investments – from traditional bank loans and commercial financing to creative approaches like seller financing, partnerships, and even international lending strategies. Whether you're buying your first duplex or raising capital for a 100-unit deal, understanding financing options will expand your possibilities and sharpen your edge as an investor.

For example, in one deal, I used a combination of a conventional bank loan and seller financing to acquire a twenty-four-unit property. The bank financed 70 percent of the purchase, while the seller agreed to carry a note for 20 percent – reducing the cash I needed to bring to the table and giving me more time to stabilize the asset. That creative structure allowed me to close quickly and preserve capital for renovations, turning a tight deal into a profitable one.

When it comes to real estate investing, one truth stands out: You don't have to use your own money to build wealth – you just need to understand how money works.

Financing is the lifeblood of real estate growth. Whether you're acquiring your first duplex or scaling into 100-unit apartment buildings, the ability to leverage other people's money (OPM) – and do it wisely – is what separates casual investors from serious wealth builders.

Let's explore the most common (and creative) financing options for multifamily properties, how to get lenders on your side, and what you need to know before signing on the dotted line.

Conventional bank loans are commonly used for smaller multifamily properties (two to four units), offering lower interest rates and longer amortization, but are typically based on personal income and credit, with higher down payment requirements and limited scalability.

Commercial real estate loans are designed for properties with five or more units and are primarily underwritten based on the property's income, offering scalable financing through local banks, credit unions, or agency lenders – with typical five to ten-year terms, DSCR requirements, and prepayment penalties that investors must navigate carefully.

For properties with more than five units, you'll typically need a commercial loan. These are underwritten based on the income the property generates, not just your personal finances.

Bridge loans are short-term, interest-only financing solutions ideal for value-add or transitional multifamily properties, offering fast funding and flexible terms for renovations or repositioning, but with higher interest rates and shorter durations that require a clear exit strategy. Bridge loans are short-term, interest-only loans used for value-add properties that need renovation or stabilization before securing permanent financing. Bridge loans are for experienced investors or those with a strong team and a defined plan.

Private and hard-money lenders offer fast, flexible financing for unique or time-sensitive deals where traditional lenders may hesitate, but their higher interest rates and short terms require careful planning and should only be used when the upside clearly justifies the cost.

Private lenders are individuals or groups who lend money at higher interest rates in exchange for speed and flexibility. Hard money lenders are professional firms that lend based on the asset, not your credit. These loans are expensive and must be used with caution.

Creative financing strategies, such as seller financing – where the seller acts as the lender and you make payments directly – can offer flexible terms and tax advantages, especially when the seller prefers steady income or wants to defer capital gains.

Seller financing allows the seller to act as the lender, with the buyer making direct monthly payments – often ideal when the seller prefers ongoing income or seeks to defer capital gains taxes.

Partnerships and joint ventures allow investors to combine resources – such as time, capital, or expertise – but require clearly defined roles, ownership structures, and exit strategies to ensure alignment and long-term success.

Equity investors are individuals or groups who contribute capital in exchange for ownership and a share of profits, while you operate the deal and they remain passive partners. For more advanced investors or larger deals, global financing tools can offer significant advantages. One example is the use of Swiss bank loans combined with interest rate swaps – sophisticated strategies that, when structured properly with expert legal and financial guidance, can unlock access to lower international interest rates. These approaches are often used by high-net-worth or international investors to reduce capital costs, hedge against rate fluctuations, and increase flexibility when acquiring or refinancing large multifamily assets. While not for beginners, these tools can dramatically shift the economics of a deal when applied strategically.

## How I Have Used Financing to Grow

Over the years, I've guided clients through seven-figure investments, each one made possible through thoughtful financing. Whether it was a traditional commercial loan for a Manhattan office building, a seller-financed duplex in Florida, or a bridge loan for a renovation project, understanding the options gave us leverage and control.

When I first stepped into real estate investing, I brought with me years of experience from the world of finance and banking – a world driven by precision, structure, and the art of leveraging capital. But it wasn't until I faced a bold opportunity – an aging Manhattan office building with strong bones and even stronger potential – that I truly understood the power of financing to unlock growth.

The building was a pre-war gem tucked between glass towers, overlooked by most but not by me. It needed vision – and capital. I didn't have millions sitting idle. What I had was clarity, a solid business case, and the knowledge that financing, used wisely, could turn this overlooked asset into a crown jewel.

That's when I secured a bridge loan.

Bridge loans aren't for the faint of heart. They come with higher rates and shorter terms, but they also offer flexibility and speed. This particular loan gave me just enough breathing room to reposition the property – update systems, modernize the common areas, and improve the tenant mix – without immediately tying up long-term financing. It was the kind of creative solution traditional lenders might shy away from, but I understood its purpose: buy time, build value, then refinance into stability.

And that's exactly what we did.

Once the improvements were made and the asset stabilized, I refinanced into a conventional loan at a much lower interest rate. That refinance unlocked equity I used to fund my next acquisition – without selling a single property. It was a textbook case of strategic leverage: turning one win into multiple opportunities, all while controlling risk and preserving upside.

What I learned in that season was this: money follows strategy. Financing isn't just a means to acquire – it's a lever to expand. It lets you move faster, scale bigger, and access deals you might otherwise pass by. But the key is understanding the fit – matching the right type of financing to the right stage of the deal.

Whether it's a bridge loan, a refinance, or creative debt structuring, the right financing is like oxygen to an investor with a clear plan. It gave me the freedom to move, to grow, and most importantly, to believe in what was possible – before the world could see it.

## What Lenders Look For

Whether it's a bank or a private capital partner, here's what matters:

- Strong business plan or pro forma
- Accurate financials and realistic rent projections
- Solid DSCR (typically 1.25+)
- Experience or strong advisory team
- Clear exit strategy

Start building relationships with lenders early – even before you have a deal in hand.

Financing isn't just about securing a loan – it's about designing a foundation for long-term, scalable success. The more informed you are about your options, the more confidently you can structure deals that align with your goals. Whether you're partnering with banks, negotiating with sellers, or exploring creative funding solutions, the right financing strategy can transform a solid opportunity into a game-changing investment.

Now it's your turn: Choose one property you're currently evaluating – or wish you were – and map out three different ways you could finance it. Use the following structure to guide your thinking:

1. Traditional Approach:
   - Loan type
   - LTV and interest rate
   - Equity required
   - Pros/Cons

2. Partnership-Based Approach:
   - Equity split (e.g., 70/30)
   - Partner role versus your role
   - Capital contributions
   - Pros/Cons

3. Creative Approach:
   - Type of creative structure (e.g., seller financing, subject-to, lease option)
   - Terms and negotiation points
   - Cash required
   - Pros/Cons

Completing this simple exercise will stretch your thinking, sharpen your strategy, and move you one step closer to your next successful deal.

## Conclusion

The right financing strategy can make or break a multifamily investment. Whether you're starting small with a conventional loan, scaling with commercial financing, or exploring advanced tools like bridge loans, partnerships, or interest rate swaps, your ability to match the deal with the right capital structure is critical to long-term success. Understanding your options – and knowing when to use them – gives you a powerful edge in a competitive market. Remember, great investors don't just find good deals – they finance them wisely to maximize cash flow, minimize risk, and build lasting wealth.

## Financing Strategies Checklist for Multifamily Real Estate

### *Understand Your Financing Options*

- Research different loan types (conventional, FHA, bridge loans, CMBS, etc.).
- Evaluate pros and cons of fixed versus variable interest rates.
- Explore government-backed programs and incentives.

### *Prepare Financial Documentation*

- Organize personal and business financial statements.
- Prepare detailed property financials including rent rolls and expense reports.
- Assemble credit history and background information.

### *Establish Relationships with Lenders*

- Identify and vet potential lenders experienced in multifamily financing.
- Build rapport and maintain open communication with lenders.
- Obtain pre-approvals or soft quotes to understand borrowing capacity.

### *Analyze Loan Terms Carefully*

- Review interest rates, fees, and amortization schedules.
- Understand prepayment penalties and loan covenants.
- Consider loan-to-value (LTV) and debt service coverage ratio (DSCR) requirements.

### *Optimize Financing Structure*

- Balance debt and equity to maximize returns while managing risk.

- Consider layering financing sources if appropriate (e.g., mezzanine loans).
- Plan refinancing opportunities to improve terms or extract equity.

### *Manage Financing Throughout Ownership*

- Monitor loan performance and compliance with lender requirements.
- Maintain strong financial records for lender reporting.
- Communicate proactively with lenders about changes or challenges.

### *Plan for Exit or Refinance*

- Understand the implications of loan terms on exit strategies.
- Prepare for refinancing by tracking market conditions and property performance.
- Work with financial advisors to optimize timing and structure.

## Reflection Questions

1. What type of financing are you most familiar with – and what types are new to you?
2. List any you'd like to learn more about (e.g., commercial loans, bridge loans, seller financing).
3. Have you spoken with a lender about your current borrowing capacity?
4. If not, who could you contact this week to start that conversation?
5. What kind of multifamily property (in terms of size and value) do you believe you can finance right now?
6. Estimate based on your available capital and leverage options.
7. What are your biggest concerns about financing real estate deals?
8. (e.g., qualifying for loans, interest rates, down

payments, risk of debt)

9. Would you rather finance deals yourself or work with partners or investors?
10. Why does that approach feel more aligned with your goals?
11. What creative financing strategies are you open to exploring?
12. (Seller financing, private money, partnerships, international lending, etc.)
13. Have you built relationships with potential lenders or mortgage brokers?
14. Who's on your financial team today – and who's missing?
15. How will you ensure that your financing aligns with your investment goals and risk tolerance?
16. What would your ideal financing structure look like for your next deal?
17. Consider the loan type, down payment, term, and expected return.
18. What is one action step you can take this week to move closer to securing financing for a future property?
19. (e.g., meet a lender, review your credit, build a pro forma, gather financials)

# CHAPTER 8:
## PART 1:THE MULTIFAMILY ACQUISITION PROCESS: NAVIGATING DEAL, DEBT, AND EQUITY

*"Success in real estate comes not just from finding great deals, but from mastering the complex dance of deal, debt, and equity."*

— Anonymous

Acquiring a multifamily property requires careful coordination of several moving parts – identifying the right investment, securing financing, and managing investor capital. Each step, from the initial property search to closing the deal, plays a crucial role in ensuring a successful and profitable transaction. Understanding the acquisition process in detail not only helps mitigate risks but also empowers investors to make informed decisions, streamline operations, and build a strong foundation for long-term portfolio growth. This chapter walks you through the key phases of the multifamily acquisition process, providing a clear road map to navigate deal, debt, and equity management effectively.

Let me take you behind the scenes of a real acquisition I'm working on right now: a 230-unit multifamily property in Lake Worth Beach, Florida. The total purchase price is $55 million, and the debt portion $39.5 million – is critical to making this deal work. In today's market, with interest rates hovering around 7 percent, the cost of capital can quickly erode returns. But here's the opportunity: the current owner locked in a loan at 5 percent, and that loan is assumable.

We're now negotiating with the bank to assume the property's existing favorable debt – an interest rate two points below current market levels. Securing that loan doesn't just save us millions over the life of the deal – it transforms the entire investment profile. Lower debt service means stronger cash flow, higher projected returns, and less pressure to overperform on operations. For equity partners, that's not just attractive – it builds trust, mitigates downside risk, and improves yield from day one. It's a powerful reminder: a great property is only half the equation. Great financing is what makes it truly work.

Understanding how to structure and secure the debt portion of your acquisition is a foundational skill for any multifamily investor. In this chapter, we'll walk through the different types of loans available, what lenders look for, how to assess your borrowing capacity, and how to negotiate terms that work for your business model.

We'll also divide the process into two clear lanes: one focused on deal and debt, and the other focused on equity raising. By approaching them as complementary yet distinct tracks, you'll gain the pacing and clarity needed to manage your acquisition more efficiently and with greater confidence.

Because when you master the capital stack – how much comes from debt and how much from equity – you position yourself as a serious investor ready to close with confidence, creativity, and structure.

## Qualifying for a Multifamily Loan

As a former commercial lender, I can tell you firsthand that borrowers who come prepared stand out. Lending is not just about paperwork and numbers; it's about trust, judgment, and risk assessment. When you apply for a multifamily loan, your lender will evaluate what we in the industry call the 3 Cs:

- **Character** – your track record, integrity, and reliability
- **Capacity** – your ability to repay the loan based on income and cash flow
- **Capital/Collateral** – the strength of your balance sheet and the value of the property

These three factors help lenders determine your creditworthiness and the risk associated with lending to you. If you understand this framework and present yourself as a low-risk, high-potential borrower, you'll move through the process more smoothly and be taken seriously as a professional investor.

Too often, aspiring investors get laser-focused on finding the perfect deal and forget that none of it matters if they can't qualify for the loan. I once coached a first-time investor who found a solid sixteen-unit property with great upside. The numbers worked, the location was strong, and the seller was motivated. But when it came time to close, the lender hesitated. His personal financials were disorganized, his credit score had recent dings, and he couldn't clearly articulate his business plan. The deal fell apart – not because the numbers didn't work, but because he wasn't positioned as a strong borrower.

Let's fix that. Below is what you need to know to qualify for a multifamily loan and build lasting credibility with lenders – from your personal financial profile to the way you present your experience and team. Because the truth is, lenders don't just underwrite properties – they underwrite people.

## Qualifying for a Multifamily Loan: What Smart Investors Know

If you are serious about buying multifamily properties, financing is a cornerstone of your success. Too often, new investors jump into deals without fully understanding what lenders expect. But you don't have to be one of them.

When you are prepared, lenders take you seriously – and the money follows.

Here's what you need to know to qualify for a multi-family loan and build long-term credibility with financing partners.

## Experience Isn't Optional – But There Are Workarounds

Lenders like a track record! If you don't have one yet, bring in a partner or mentor who does. Teaming up shows lenders you're taking the process seriously and reduces their risk. I have seen first-time buyers get funding because they align themselves with experienced sponsors. Relationships matter.

## Net Worth and Liquidity Are More Than Numbers

As a rule of thumb:

- Your net worth should match or exceed the loan amount.
- Your liquidity (money you can access quickly) should be 10 to 20 percent of the loan amount after closing.

Example: For a $4 million loan, aim for $4 million in net worth and $400,000 to $800,000 in liquid assets after the deal closes.

## Your Credit Score Tells a Story – Make Sure It's a Good One

Although investors and lenders focus heavily on the deal's cash flow for loan repayment, your personal credit history still plays a critical role. It should reflect financial stability, responsible debt management, and the absence of recent bankruptcies or foreclosures. If your credit score is below the ideal range, take proactive steps to strengthen it before applying for financing – doing so will improve your credibility and negotiating power.

## Put Skin in the Game – Down Payment Matters

Most lenders require 25 percent to 30 percent down. If you are syndicating the deal, that equity might come from investor partners, but you still need to show your commitment. Lenders love to see that you are financially and emotionally invested. So do your partners.

## Understand DSCR – Lenders Live by It

Your **Debt Service Coverage Ratio (DSCR)** must usually be between **1.20x and 1.30x**. This simply means your net income should be 20 percent to 30 percent higher than your annual debt obligations.

**Formula:** Net Operating Income ÷ Annual Debt Service

Example: If your NOI is $150,000 and your annual debt payment is $120,000, your DSCR is 1.25x – right where it should be.

If the loan is recourse (you personally guarantee it), lenders will also evaluate your entire financial profile – including income, expenses, and existing liabilities – to determine whether you can absorb setbacks.

## Lenders Are Not Just Money – They're a Strategic Asset

Your lender isn't just a funding source – they're a key strategic partner in your business. The right lender brings more than money to the table. They help you structure smarter deals, flag potential risks before they become problems, and guide you through shifting market conditions. A great lender understands your long-term vision and works with you to grow, not just close. When you treat your lender as part of your team – not just a transaction – you build relationships that can unlock better terms, faster approvals, and more opportunities down the line.

Here's a quick comparison I often use to help clients decide which path fits their strategy and timeline.

- Fannie Mae / Freddie Mac

- o *Best For:* Long-term, stabilized deals
  - o *Pros:* Low rates, non-recourse options
- Bank Loans
  - o *Best For:* Smaller or local deals
  - o *Pros:* Relationship-driven, flexible
- Bridge Loans
  - o *Best For:* Value-add opportunities
  - o *Pros:* Higher leverage, interest-only
- CMBS (Commercial Mortgage-Backed Securities)
  - o *Best For:* Large, institutional deals
  - o *Pros:* Long terms, fixed rates
- Private Lenders
  - o *Best For:* Fast, opportunistic deals
  - o *Pros:* Speed, flexibility, creativity

## The Multifamily Acquisition Process Requires the Ability to Navigate the Deal, Debt, and Equity

### *Step 1: Property Identification and Preliminary Analysis*

- Identify properties that meet your acquisition criteria.
- Tour the property and visit rent comparables in the area to assess market rents.
- Conduct an initial underwriting to estimate potential returns and risks.
- Discuss questions and concerns with your broker to clarify details.

### *Step 2: Debt Financing Soft Quote*

- Obtain an initial soft quote from your lender regarding potential loan terms.
- Use this information to refine your underwriting and purchase offer.

### *Step 3: Letter of Intent (LOI)*

- Submit a Letter of Intent to the seller outlining your proposed purchase terms.
- Negotiate the LOI terms as needed with the seller.
- Update your debt quote if necessary to reflect changes in terms.

### *Step 4: Due Diligence Preparation*

- Upon selection as the best and final bidder, get lender buy-in for the loan.
- Complete the buyer questionnaire and participate in the buyer interview.
- Negotiate final terms to be awarded the deal.
- Prepare the purchase agreement with your real estate attorney.

### *Step 5: Loan Application and Legal Documentation*

- Move forward with the loan application process.
- Provide your attorney with all required information to prepare the Private Placement Memorandum (PPM), Operating Agreement (OA), Subscription Agreement (SA), SEC filings, and Blue Sky filings.
- Negotiate and finalize the purchase agreement.
- Identify third-party vendors for reports such as environmental, structural, and appraisal.
- Prepare an investment summary for potential equity investors.
- Notify the management company to plan for due diligence.

### *Step 6: Investor Outreach and Due Diligence*

- Begin discussions with potential equity investors through webinars and meetings.
- Set up bank accounts and collect investor funds.

- Conduct financial due diligence, including lease file audits and seller financial verification.
- Provide the lender with the purchase agreement, personal financial statements, schedules, organizational documents, underwriting reports, bios, and business plans.
- Continue legal and title due diligence.
- Schedule third-party inspections and reports.
- Revise legal documents and pitch materials as necessary.

## Step 7: Finalizing Deal, Debt, and Equity

- Sign off on due diligence or, if necessary, attempt to renegotiate (re-trade) or cancel the deal.
- Obtain a commitment letter from the lender.
- Send the balance of the earnest money deposit.
- Lock in the interest rate with the lender.
- Complete raising and collecting all investor funds.
- Finalize last-minute deal, legal, and lender requirements.
- Finalize Blue Sky filings and settlement statements.
- Send all necessary funds to the closing agent.

## Step 8: Closing and Post-Closing

- Close the deal successfully.
- Transfer security deposits and working capital to the property management company.
- The lender returns the rate lock and other deposits.
- Maintain clear communication with investors.
- Thank everyone who helped close the deal. Every deal is a team effort, and acknowledging the people who helped bring it to life – your lender who fought for better terms, your attorney who

caught a crucial clause, your investors who trusted your vision, and your property manager already working to stabilize the asset – builds loyalty and respect. Thoughtful recognition doesn't just show professionalism; it strengthens your reputation and keeps great people excited to work with you on the next one.

Mastering the multifamily acquisition process is essential for building a successful real estate portfolio. By carefully navigating each step – from property identification and underwriting to securing financing and managing investor capital – you set the stage for profitable investments and long-term growth. Staying organized, communicating clearly with all parties, and remaining adaptable to challenges will help you close deals efficiently and confidently. Remember, every acquisition is not just a transaction but a strategic move toward your broader investment goals and legacy.

## Conclusion

Acquiring a multifamily property is a complex but rewarding process that requires strategic coordination of the deal, the debt, and the equity. From identifying the right opportunity to securing financing and aligning with investors, each step demands clarity, due diligence, and execution. Success lies in your ability to manage the moving parts – balancing speed with precision, relationships with analysis, and vision with structure. When done right, the acquisition process is not just a transaction – it's the foundation of long-term growth, cash flow, and value creation.

Let's Connect. If you would like help with preparing your financing package, improving your borrower profile, or simply want to better understand your loan options, I invite you to reach out. Whether you're just starting out or ready to scale up, I'm here to guide you with the insight of a former commercial lender and the perspective of an active multifamily investor. Email me at mellis@fsacap.com to schedule a free consultation.

## Reflection Questions

1. Where do I currently stand in terms of net worth and liquidity? Am I ready to apply for a multi-family loan, or do I need to build up resources first?
2. Do I have the experience – or access to someone who does – to meet lender expectations? If not, who can I partner with?
3. Is my credit profile aligned with my goals? What steps can I take today to strengthen it?
4. Do I treat my lender as a transactional contact or as part of my long-term investment team?
5. Have I selected the best loan structure for the type of property I want to acquire and the strategy I'm following?.

# CHAPTER 8:
## PART 2: THE MULTIFAMILY ACQUISITION PROCESS: RAISE EQUITY FOR MULTIFAMILY INVESTMENTS

*"Raising equity isn't about asking for money — it's about offering opportunity. When you align vision with value, the right investors will follow."*

— Maria L. Ellis

Raising equity isn't just about capital — it's about conviction. When someone invests in your deal, they're really investing in your clarity, credibility, and confidence.

It requires the ability to clearly communicate your vision, structure deals transparently, and build trust with potential investors — whether they're family offices, institutional players, or individual accredited investors. Equity is more than just capital; it's partnership. When done right, raising equity allows you to scale faster, spread risk, and attract the kind of investors who not only fund your deals but champion your long-term vision.

When you master the capital stack — how much comes from debt and how much from equity — you position yourself as a serious investor ready to close with confidence, creativity, and structure. But remember, who you invite into your deal matters just as much as how you structure it. Finding the right limited partners/investors is critical — not only because they contribute capital but because they become part of your investment ecosystem. You want limited partners who believe in your vision, respect your leadership, and are committed to long-term value creation, not just short-term gains.

As the general partner (GP), you'll lead the acquisition, financing, and management strategy – but you don't have to do it alone. Consider bringing in one or two additional general partners who complement your strengths. These might include an experienced underwriter, a capital raiser with investor relationships, or a property management expert who knows the local market inside and out. When your GP team brings a balanced mix of skills – deal sourcing, operations, finance, investor relations – you increase your credibility, execution power, and overall deal success. Multifamily investing is a team sport. Structure your capital stack with intention – and choose your team with equal precision.

Once you have found a promising multifamily deal and understand your financing options, the next step is often the most personal: raising equity capital. This is where you bring in investors to cover the down payment, capital expenditures, and other deal-related costs not covered by the loan. The following are some keyways to raise equity for multifamily investments.

## Friends and Family

A common starting point, especially for newer investors. Treat friends-and-family money like institutional capital. Informal relationships become liabilities fast when expectations aren't documented in writing.

## High-Net-Worth Individuals

Accredited investors are looking for strong returns and passive income. Offer a clear value proposition, including projected cash flow, IRR, exit strategy, and your experience as the operator.

## Joint Ventures (JVs)

In a JV, two or more parties come together with capital and operational roles defined. This is a great fit for larger deals where equity is pooled from fewer players who want more control.

## Syndications

A syndication allows you to raise equity from multiple passive investors. You serve as the General Partner (GP), and they become Limited Partners (LPs). This structure comes with strict SEC compliance requirements, so it must be done correctly.

## Private Equity and Institutional Capital

For larger portfolios or experienced operators, private equity firms may contribute sizable equity. This route requires a track record, sophistication, and often a co-investment from you.

**What to watch out for** includes overpromising returns, failing to disclose risks, structuring vague or unclear deals, and improperly raising funds from personal relationships – all of which can lead to legal trouble, damaged credibility, and failed investments if not handled with transparency, professionalism, and proper compliance. Always underwrite conservatively. Never promise guaranteed returns. Investors must understand the risks. Failing to disclose material risks can expose you to legal liabilities. Unclear equity splits, vague roles, and loose payout terms don't just cause confusion – they kill trust and stall deals. If you're raising money from friends, it still qualifies as selling security and must be handled with care.

## Hire the Right Attorney – Not Just Any Attorney

When it comes to raising equity, you're no longer just buying real estate – you are issuing security under federal and state laws. This is why hiring a real estate attorney who specializes in multifamily syndications and understands SEC compliance is non-negotiable.

A qualified attorney will help structure your deal correctly (JV versus syndication), draft your Private Placement Memorandum (PPM), ensure you comply with SEC exemptions (506(b) versus 506(c)),and protect you and your investors with solid operating agreements and disclosures. I have seen deals with great potential fall apart because investors didn't retain the right legal guidance. You might save money upfront by skipping legal counsel, but you will pay dearly later if something goes wrong.

Raising equity is about more than just money – it's about building trust and creating long-term relationships. Investors want to know you're professional, transparent, and legally sound. Respect their capital, protect their interests, and run your deals with integrity, and you'll never have trouble raising equity again.

## Equity Raising Guide: How to Raise Capital for Your Multifamily Deal

Whether you're syndicating your first deal or expanding your portfolio, raising equity is one of the most important (and relationship-driven) skills you'll develop as a multifamily investor. Done right, it builds lasting trust. Done wrong, it creates liability and reputational damage. This guide helps you do it right – from preparation to closing.

## Step 1: Prepare Before You Pitch

*Know Your Deal Inside and Out*

- Property type, location, unit count, market comps
- Business plan: value-add? renovation? cash-flow play?
- Hold period, projected returns, exit strategy

**Know Your Numbers**

- Total capital raise required
- Projected IRR, cash-on-cash, and equity multiple
- Sponsor fees (acquisition, asset management,

etc.)

## Step 2: Identify Your Ideal Investors

- Friends and Family – Start here but treat them like investors, not donors
- Accredited Investors – High-net-worth individuals looking for passive income
- JV Partners – More active involvement, fewer investors
- Syndication LPs – Passive, diversified capital pool
- Private Equity – Institutional capital (for experienced operators)

## Step 3: Structure the Deal Correctly

*Choose Your Model*

- Joint Venture (JV) – Shared control, fewer investors
- Syndication (LP/GP Structure) – You're the operator (GP); they're passive (LPs)

*Work With a Qualified Attorney:*

- Draft a Private Placement Memorandum (PPM)
- Set up the operating agreement and subscription docs
- Ensure compliance with SEC rules (Reg D: 506(b) versus 506(c))
- If you cut corners on legal, you cut the throat of your deal. Hire a syndication attorney.

*Communicate Professionally*

*Create an Investor Package*

- Executive summary (two to three pages)
- Full investor deck (market, team, financials, strategy)
- PPM and legal documents

### *Deliver with Confidence*

- Walk through the opportunity with honesty and clarity.
- Confidence is earned through preparation, not persuasion.
- Invite questions. Don't dodge objections – welcome them as buying signals.

## Step 5: Raise Capital and Close

- Track soft commitments (verbal yes) versus hard commitments (funds wired)
- Use a secure investor portal or tracking sheet
- Keep investors informed on deal progress
- Be upfront about deadlines. Capital raises with urgency and clarity move faster.

### *Pitfalls to Avoid*

- Making guarantees – You can project returns but never promise them.
- Accepting funds without legal docs – Always use proper subscription agreements.
- Overcomplicating the structure – Keep it simple and easy to explain.
- Ignoring SEC rules – Even with friends or family, compliance is essential.

### *Pro Tip: Build Long-Term Trust*

- Deliver clear, timely investor updates after the deal closes
- Communicate openly about progress, wins, and setbacks
- Distribute returns on time and according to the operating agreement
- Treat every investor like a partner in your business

## Conclusion

Raising equity is both an art and a science – blending

trust, transparency, and relationship-building with a strong command of financials, market data, and deal structure. Investors aren't just looking for high returns; they're looking for confidence in the operator, clarity in the business plan, and alignment in values and expectations. They want to know their capital is protected, their questions will be answered, and that you can execute the vision with integrity and discipline. The most successful capital raisers tell a compelling story backed by solid numbers, communicate consistently, and treat investor relationships as long-term partnerships. Mastering this balance not only unlocks capital – it builds a loyal investor base ready to grow with you deal after deal.

## Equity Raising Checklist

Use this before launching your next capital raise:

- Defined the deal and capital needs clearly
- Identified ideal investor profiles
- Hired a multifamily real estate attorney
- Created pitch materials (summary, deck, PPM)
- Determined appropriate SEC exemption (506(b) or 506(c))
- Set up a tracking system for commitments and funds
- Practiced your pitch and investor Q&A
- Scheduled regular updates and a communication plan post-close

## Reflection Questions: Raising Equity for Multifamily Investments

Use these questions to reflect on your readiness, refine your approach, and improve your future equity raises.

### *Mindset and Preparation*

1. What fears or limiting beliefs do I have around asking others for money – and how might those beliefs be holding me back?

2. How confident am I in presenting a multifamily deal to potential investors? What would help increase that confidence?

3. Have I clearly defined the type of deals I want to pursue and the kind of investors I want to attract?

### Investor Relations

4. Who in my current network could be a potential investor or refer me to one?

5. What can I do to build trust with investors beyond the numbers – through education, transparency, or consistent communication?

6. How can I make my next investor pitch feel more like a conversation and less like a sales pitch?

### Legal and Compliance

7. Do I fully understand the legal requirements around raising capital? If not, who can I bring onto my team to help guide me?

8. Have I hired an attorney who specializes in multifamily and SEC-compliant syndications – or am I relying on general legal advice?

### Deal Structuring and Communication

9. How simple and understandable is my deal structure to someone unfamiliar with real estate investing?

10. What could I improve in my investor pitch materials – my executive summary, slide deck, or financial projections?

11. Have I reviewed my past raises (if applicable) to identify what worked, what didn't, and what I can do better?

### Long-Term Perspective

12. How am I nurturing long-term relationships with my current or potential investors between deals?

13. What systems do I have in place to track inves-

tor commitments, communication, and performance?

14. What would success look like for me over the next twelve to twenty-four months in terms of equity raised, deals closed, and investor relationships built?

15. Am I presenting myself not just as a dealmaker, but as a steward of other people's capital – with integrity, strategy, and vision?

## Building the Foundation for Long-Term Success

Acquiring a multifamily property is never just about the building – it's about the strategy behind the numbers, the people behind the capital, and the systems behind the growth. Navigating the deal, securing smart debt, and raising equity from the right investors are the three pillars of a successful acquisition – and each one requires clarity, preparation, and integrity.

As a former commercial lender and now a multifamily investor, I've learned that the real power lies in how you approach the process: with transparency, discipline, and a long-term mindset. The more prepared and professional you are, the more trust you build – and in this business, trust is your greatest asset.

Whether you're raising your first dollar or structuring your next million, remember this: deals come and go, but your reputation and relationships will carry you through every market cycle. Build them wisely.

At the risk of being repetitive, pay close attention to the checklist and reflection questions provided at the end of this chapter. They are not just exercises – they're tools to help you make smarter decisions, avoid costly mistakes, and step into your role as a confident, capable multifamily investor.

Let this chapter be your blueprint – and your reminder – that you're not just acquiring assets. You're building a legacy.

### Property Identification and Preliminary Analysis

- o Identify properties meeting your acquisition criteria.
- o Tour the property and analyze local rent comparables.
- o Conduct initial underwriting to assess returns and risks.
- o Discuss details and questions with your broker.

### Debt Financing

- o Obtain a soft quote from lenders for preliminary loan terms.
- o Refine underwriting and purchase offer based on lender feedback.

### Letter of Intent (LOI)

- o Submit LOI outlining proposed purchase terms.
- o Negotiate LOI terms with the seller as needed.
- o Update debt quote to reflect negotiated terms.

### Due Diligence Preparation

- o Get lender buy-in upon selection as the best bidder.
- o Complete buyer questionnaires and interviews.
- o Negotiate and finalize the purchase agreement with an attorney.

### Loan Application and Legal Documentation

- o Proceed with the loan application process.
- o Provide your attorney with required information for legal documents and filings including Private Placement Memorandum (PPM), Operating Agreement (OA), Subscription Agreement (SA), SEC filings, and

Blue Sky filings.

### *Prepare investment summary for equity investors.*

- o Notify the management company to prepare for due diligence.
- o Investor Outreach and Due Diligence
- o Engage equity investors via meetings and webinars.
- o Set up bank accounts and collect investor funds.
- o Conduct thorough financial and legal due diligence.
- o Update legal and pitch documents as needed.

### *Finalizing Deal, Debt, and Equity*

- o Sign off on due diligence or negotiate deal terms further.
- o Obtain lender commitment letter.
- o Submit earnest money deposits and lock interest rates.
- o Complete equity raise and finalize lender requirements.

### *Prepare for closing with all legal filings and settlement statements.*

- o Closing and Post-Closing
- o Close the transaction successfully.
- o Transfer security deposits and working capital to the management company.
- o Communicate closing details and ongoing updates with investors.
- o Acknowledge and thank all contributors to the deal.

## Reflection Questions

1. How well do you understand each step of the multifamily acquisition process? Where do you feel most confident, and where do you need further knowledge or support?

2. What criteria do you use to identify potential properties that fit your investment goals?
3. How do you incorporate lender feedback into your underwriting and offer strategies?
4. What is your approach to negotiating Letters of Intent and purchase agreements?
5. How thorough is your due diligence process? What tools or professionals do you rely on to conduct inspections and financial reviews?
6. How do you manage communication and coordination among brokers, lenders, attorneys, and investors during the acquisition?
7. What challenges have you faced or anticipate in raising equity and coordinating investor relations?
8. How do you prepare for closing to ensure a smooth transition post-acquisition?
9. What lessons have you learned from past acquisitions that will improve your process going forward?
10. What is one action step you can take to strengthen your multifamily acquisition skills today?

# CHAPTER 9:
# BUILDING A WORLD-CLASS INVESTMENT TEAM

*"If you want to go fast, go alone. If you*
*want to go far, go together."*
— African Proverb

Let's start with a simple truth: a great deal means nothing without the right team to execute it.

Years ago, I learned the hard way just how essential a good attorney can be. We were ready to close when a critical title issue popped up. My first attorney missed it completely. It wasn't until I brought in a more experienced real estate lawyer that the issue was spotted and resolved – just in time. Without that second opinion, we could have inherited a legal headache that would have cost us tens of thousands. Remember, building the right team is not optional – it's fundamental.

In this chapter, you'll learn who you need on your team – from brokers and lenders to attorneys, contractors, and property managers – and how to find, vet, and collaborate with them effectively. The goal isn't just to delegate tasks, but to create a partnership culture built on trust, communication, and aligned goals. When you build wisely, your team becomes your greatest asset.

Behind every successful investor is a strong support system. Real estate may offer freedom, but it's not meant to be done alone. Whether you're managing your first property or closing on a multi-million-dollar acquisition, the right team can save you time, protect your investment, and open doors to opportunities you couldn't access on your own.

One of the biggest myths in real estate investing is that you have to do everything yourself.

The truth? Successful investors don't go it alone – they build strong teams. Whether you're buying your first duplex or closing on a 100-unit apartment complex, the people you surround yourself with will determine how fast you grow, how smoothly your deals run, and how much value you can extract from your investments.

I've seen firsthand how the right team can turn an average deal into a winning investment – and how the wrong team can sink even the most promising opportunity.

In this chapter, we'll break down the essential members of a real estate investment team, how to find them, how to vet them, and how to cultivate long-term partnerships that support your goals.

## The Core Members of Your Investment Team

The real estate broker or agent – ideally specialized in multifamily or investment properties – is your frontline ally in sourcing deals, offering not just listings but local market insight, investor-focused experience, and access to off-market opportunities that align with your investment goals.

A mortgage broker or commercial lender plays a critical role in structuring your financing and securing the most favorable loan terms for your multifamily investment. The right professional doesn't just find a loan – they find the right loan, tailored to your deal's size, condition, and financial profile. A seasoned broker with multifamily experience understands key metrics like Debt Service Coverage Ratio (DSCR), can navigate complex underwriting processes, and ensures your financing aligns with your acquisition timeline. Their access to a wide network of lenders – including banks, credit unions, and agency sources – can save you tens of thousands in interest and fees over the life of the loan, making them a vital member of your investment team.

Real estate attorney is your legal shield, ensuring your interests are protected through contract review, entity formation, and regulatory compliance, particularly in complex multifamily transactions involving syndications, SEC filings, and local property laws. Your attorney is your legal shield – reviewing contracts, helping you form entities (like LLCs), and protecting your interests during negotiations and closings.

Property manager is essential if you're not managing the day-to-day operations yourself, providing oversight on leasing, maintenance, rent collection, and tenant relations – so choose one with experience in similar multifamily properties, strong communication systems, and trusted local vendor networks. If you don't plan to manage tenants, rent collection, maintenance, and leasing yourself, you'll need a reliable property management company.

CPA or real estate-savvy accountant is vital to maximizing your returns through smart tax strategies like depreciation, cost segregation, and 1031 exchanges – so seek one with multifamily experience, knowledge of passive income rules, and a proactive, strategic approach. Taxes can make or break your returns. Your accountant should help you plan for depreciation, capital gains, 1031 exchanges, cost segregation, and more.

General contractor or handyman is essential for value-add projects and renovations, ensuring work is completed efficiently, safely, and within budget – so choose someone with a solid track record, proper credentials, and transparent, written agreements. If you're doing value-add projects or renovations, this person will be crucial. A dependable contractor ensures work gets done on time, on budget, and up to code.

Knowledgeable insurance agent is crucial to safeguarding your property, liability, and rental income, so work with someone experienced in multifamily coverage who understands varying risk profiles and can clearly explain your protection options. Look for a multifamily insurance policy that covers the structure, general liability, and loss of rental income.

Mentor, advisor, or investment partner can accelerate your growth and reduce costly mistakes by offering guidance grounded in real-world experience – so seek someone who shares your values, communicates honestly, and has a proven, ethical track record in multifamily investing. My first mentor had twenty years of experience in multifamily and saved me from overleveraging on my second deal.

## How I Built My Team

My transition from finance to real estate taught me the value of delegation and collaboration. I learned this lesson firsthand as I began to build my own multifamily team. At first, I tried to do everything myself – finding deals, analyzing numbers, managing renovations – but I quickly hit a wall. There simply weren't enough hours in the day, and I knew I needed people around me who could complement my strengths and cover my weaknesses.

My first key hire was a broker who specialized in multifamily deals. She introduced me to a six-unit property in Miami that wasn't even on the market yet.

That one connection led to our first successful acquisition – a mid-sized multifamily in a growing neighborhood.

Next, I brought on an underwriter who helped us dig deeper into the numbers. He flagged things I might have missed, and together we developed a more disciplined and data-driven investment approach. After that, I partnered with a seasoned construction manager who had walked hundreds of units and could tell within minutes what a rehab would really cost. His insight saved us from underestimating renovation budgets – and from overpaying.

As we grew, I added a property manager who shared our values and treated tenants with care and respect. She helped stabilize occupancy, cut turnover, and build community. And perhaps most importantly, I connected with a few equity partners who believed in our vision and were willing to invest not just money, but trust.

That's how my team was built – not all at once, but one relationship at a time. One brought access to deals, another underwriting precision, and another on-the-ground renovation oversight.

Together, we created something far bigger than I could've done alone.

Over time, I built a team I could trust – brokers who brought me quality deals, property managers who kept my tenants happy, and attorneys who protected me from costly errors. I also mentored and was mentored, learning from others who had walked this path before.

Your team is your leverage. They allow you to scale, reduce stress, and stay in your zone of genius.

Tips for vetting and managing your team include checking references, starting with small projects, using clear written agreements, maintaining regular communication, and rewarding reliability – because building a trustworthy, high-performing team is essential to long-term success in multifamily investing.

The strength of your real estate business depends on the strength of your relationships. A world-class team doesn't just help you close deals; they help you avoid mistakes, scale with confidence, and navigate the unexpected. Whether you're just beginning to build that team or refining one already in place, remember this: trust, communication, and shared vision are more valuable than any spreadsheet or appraisal. In the next chapter, we'll dive into how to effectively manage your properties after you've acquired them – because buying the building is just the beginning. Managing for profit and performance is where real wealth is created.

## Building a World-Class Investment Team Checklist

### *Identify Key Roles*

- Define essential team roles: property manager, broker, lender, attorney, accountant, contractor, and mentor/advisor.
- Determine which roles you will fill personally and which to outsource or delegate.

### *Recruit Qualified Professionals*

- Vet candidates thoroughly through interviews, references, and past performance.
- Seek team members with relevant experience in multifamily real estate.
- Prioritize professionals who align with your investment philosophy and goals.

### *Establish Clear Expectations*

- Define roles and responsibilities for each team member.
- Set performance standards and measurable goals.
- Communicate expectations clearly during onboarding and ongoing meetings.

### *Foster Effective Communication*

- Schedule regular team meetings and updates.
- Use collaboration tools (e.g., email, project management apps) to keep everyone aligned.
- Encourage open feedback and problem-solving discussions.

### *Build Trust and Accountability*

- Create a culture of transparency and reliability.
- Monitor progress and provide constructive feedback.
- Recognize and reward strong performance and contributions.

### *Invest in Team Development*

- Provide training and educational opportunities to enhance skills.
- Encourage attendance at industry conferences and networking events.
- Promote mentorship and knowledge sharing within the team.

### *Review and Optimize Team Performance*

- Conduct periodic evaluations of team effectiveness and fit.
- Address conflicts or performance issues promptly.
- Adjust team composition as portfolio and needs evolve.

## Core Interview Questions for your Team Members

### *Experience and Expertise*

1. Can you describe your experience with multifamily properties similar to those in my portfolio?
2. What is the largest or most complex multifamily deal/project you have handled?
3. How do you stay current with real estate market trends, laws, and best practices?
4. Can you share examples of challenges you've encountered and how you resolved them?

### *Process and Approach*

5. How do you approach tenant screening, leasing, or deal negotiations (customize per role)?
6. What tools or software do you use to manage your workflow and communicate with clients?
7. How do you ensure compliance with relevant regulations and avoid legal risks?
8. How do you prioritize tasks when managing

multiple properties or clients?

## Communication and Relationship Management

9. How often and through which channels do you communicate progress or updates to your clients?
10. How do you handle conflicts or disagreements with clients, tenants, or vendors?
11. What steps do you take to build trust and maintain long-term relationships with your clients?

## References and Performance

12. Can you provide references from at least three clients you have worked with recently?
13. How do you measure your success or effectiveness in your role?
14. What differentiates you from others in your profession?

## Red Flags to Watch For

- Hesitation or vagueness in answers.
- Refusal or delay in providing references.
- Lack of clear examples or measurable results.
- Negative or inconsistent feedback from references.
- Unprofessional behavior or poor communication during the interview.

## Post-Interview Evaluation Checklist

- Did the candidate demonstrate relevant multifamily experience?
- Were they knowledgeable about market conditions and regulations?
- Did their communication style align with your expectations?
- Were their references positive and credible?
- Do the candidate's values and approach fit with your team culture?

- Are you confident in their ability to deliver results?

## Conclusion

In this chapter, you have learned who you need on your team – from brokers and lenders to attorneys, contractors, and property managers – and how to find, vet, and collaborate with them effectively. The goal isn't just to delegate tasks but to create a partnership culture built on trust, communication, and aligned goals. When you build wisely, your team becomes your greatest asset. Remember, the purpose of building a strong team isn't just about executing tasks – it's about scaling your vision. The right partners allow you to go further, faster. They bring perspective, protect your blind spots, and multiply your efforts – like when my broker and CPA caught a tax liability I would've missed.

Leveraging other people's time, expertise, and networks is how you preserve your time, reduce risk, and build sustainable, generational wealth. Don't just think in terms of roles – think in terms of relationships that grow with your business and amplify your long-term impact.

## Reflection Questions

1. Which of the key team roles do you already have filled?
2. (Broker, lender, attorney, property manager, etc.) List their names or companies.
3. Which roles are still missing or need to be upgraded?
4. Where are the biggest gaps or weak links in your current team?
5. What qualities do you value most in your professional partners?
6. (e.g., responsiveness, expertise, transparency, shared values)
7. Who in your current network could introduce

you to high-quality team members?

8. (e.g., real estate groups, mentors, other investors)
9. Have you clearly defined what you expect from each team member?
10. If not, how can you improve communication and alignment?
11. How will you vet new professionals before bringing them into your team?
12. What questions will you ask? What red flags will you look for?
13. Have you documented your standard processes for working with your team?
14. (e.g., deal review steps, communication protocols, renovation timelines)
15. Which member of your team will be your "first call" when you have a potential deal?
16. Why?
17. What lessons have you learned – positive or negative – from past partnerships or contractor experiences?
18. What is one action step you can take this week to strengthen your team or fill a missing role?

# CHAPTER 10:
# TAX STRATEGIES FOR MULTIFAMILY INVESTORS – MAXIMIZING AFTER-TAX RETURNS

*"Smart investors know that maximizing returns isn't just about what you make, but what you keep."*
— Anonymous

Investing in multifamily real estate offers not only the potential for steady cash flow and long-term appreciation but also powerful tax advantages that can significantly enhance your overall returns. Understanding how to leverage these benefits – from deductions and depreciation to 1031 exchanges and beyond – is essential for maximizing your after-tax profits and building lasting wealth.

Let me share a story that brings this to life. A few years ago, one of my investor friends, Linda, proudly told me about a multifamily deal she'd just exited. She'd made a sizable gain and was thrilled – until her CPA called to tell her about the massive tax bill coming her way. Linda had focused so much on growing her return that she forgot to structure the exit in a tax-efficient way. The result? She gave away a huge chunk of her profits to the IRS.

Contrast that with another client, Marcus, who planned his exit in advance. He used a cost segregation study, accelerated depreciation, and ultimately did a 1031 exchange into a larger asset. Not only did he defer taxes, but he expanded his portfolio and increased his cash flow.

Similar gains, wildly different outcomes. These stories highlight why tax strategy isn't just an afterthought. It's a core part of smart investing.

In this chapter, we'll break down the key tax advantages available to multifamily investors: depreciation, cost segregation, 1031 exchanges, bonus depreciation, passive loss rules, and more. But rather than just listing the terms, we'll show you how and when to use each of them to your advantage.

Because when you understand how to legally minimize taxes, you free up more capital to reinvest, grow your portfolio faster, and protect your wealth for the long term.

This chapter demystifies the key tax strategies available to multifamily investors and explains how to use them effectively within your investment plan.

## Understanding Tax Deductions

One of the most immediate benefits of owning multifamily properties is the ability to deduct many expenses against your rental income, reducing your taxable income:

Operating Expenses: Property management fees, maintenance costs, repairs, utilities, insurance, and property taxes are all deductible in the year they are incurred.

Mortgage Interest: Interest paid on loans used to acquire or improve the property is deductible, often constituting a large portion of deductions, especially early in ownership.

Professional Fees: Legal, accounting, and consulting fees related to the property are also deductible.

Travel Expenses: If you travel to your property for management or maintenance, associated travel costs can be deductible.

Maximizing deductions means careful record-keeping and working with tax professionals to ensure you capture all allowable expenses. These deductions reduce your taxable rental income, thereby improving your cash flow after taxes.

## Depreciation: A Powerful Non-Cash Deduction

Depreciation is a unique tax advantage that allows you to deduct a portion of the property's value each year, reflecting the wear and tear over time – even though no cash is actually spent in those years.

The IRS currently allows residential rental properties to be depreciated over twenty-seven-and-a-half years using the straight-line method. Depreciation reduces your taxable income without affecting your cash flow, as it's a non-cash expense. You can also depreciate certain components (like appliances or carpeting) over shorter lives using cost segregation studies – an advanced strategy to accelerate deductions in the early years.

Example: If you purchase a multifamily property for $1 million (with a land value of $200,000 and a building value of $800,000), your annual depreciation deduction would be approximately $29,090 ($800,000 ÷ 27.5).

Depreciation can significantly lower your tax bill, especially in the early years of ownership, but be mindful of depreciation recapture taxes when you sell (discussed later).

## Passive Activity Losses and Real Estate Professional Status

Typically, rental real estate income is considered passive, meaning losses from the property can only offset passive income – not active income like wages – limiting your ability to use losses to reduce taxes on your day job.

However, there are important exceptions: If your income is below certain thresholds, you may qualify to deduct up to $25,000 of rental losses against non-passive income due to the active participation exception. If you or your spouse qualify as a real estate professional (spending more than 750 hours per year materially participating in real estate activities), you can deduct rental losses fully against other income.

When you structure your ownership and involvement strategically – with tax rules in mind – you can significantly enhance your overall returns by maximizing available tax benefits.

## 1031 Exchanges: Deferring Capital Gains Taxes

As detailed in Chapter 17, a 1031 exchange lets you defer capital gains taxes when you sell one investment property and reinvest in another "like-kind" property. This strategy preserves your capital, allowing you to reinvest the full sale proceeds into a new property. 1031 exchanges are a cornerstone of multifamily investors' tax planning, enabling portfolio growth without immediate tax consequences. Remember, strict timelines and rules apply – you must identify replacement properties within forty-five days and close within 180 days.

Using 1031 exchanges strategically can multiply your wealth over time by keeping more of your money working for you.

## Cost Segregation Studies

A cost segregation study breaks down your property's purchase price into different components with shorter depreciation lives (like personal property or land improvements).

This accelerates depreciation deductions, front-loading your tax benefits into the early years of ownership. It can create significant upfront tax savings and improve your cash flow. Typically done by specialized engineers or consultants, it's most beneficial for higher-value properties or new construction. This advanced tax strategy requires professional expertise but can be a powerful tool for maximizing after-tax returns.

## Opportunity Zones and Other Incentives

Investors may also benefit from special tax incentives such as Opportunity Zones, which provide tax deferrals and exclusions for investments in designated economically distressed areas. By investing capital gains into Opportunity Zone Funds, you can defer tax on those gains and potentially exclude gains from the Opportunity Zone investment if held long-term. Other local or state tax incentives may apply depending on the property's location. Stay informed about these programs, as they can offer substantial tax savings in certain circumstances.

I will share another powerful example – this time about Opportunity Zones. Several years ago, a colleague of mine, Daniel, sold a commercial property and was staring down a massive capital gains tax bill. He started exploring options to reduce the tax hit and discovered the Opportunity Zone program. After doing some research, Daniel invested those capital gains into an Opportunity Zone Fund focused on redeveloping mixed-use properties in an economically distressed downtown area.

Because of the investment structure, Daniel was able to defer the taxes on his original gains for several years. Even better, since he planned to hold the Opportunity Zone asset for more than ten years, he became eligible to completely exclude the gains from the new investment. The property appreciated significantly while revitalizing the neighborhood – and Daniel kept more of the upside.

It's the kind of strategy many investors overlook – not because it doesn't work, but because it demands upfront planning and the curiosity to learn something new. But for those willing to go the extra mile, the payoff can be substantial.

Opportunity Zones are just one example. Depending on the location of your property, you may also qualify for state or local tax incentives, rehabilitation credits, or green energy rebates. These programs change over time, so it's essential to stay informed and work with professionals who track these opportunities.

When you layer these incentives onto a solid multifamily deal, you're not just investing – you're multiplying your outcomes.

## Depreciation Recapture and Capital Gains Taxes

When you sell your multifamily property, you must pay taxes on the gain, which includes Capital Gains Tax: Taxed at long-term rates if held over a year, generally 15 to 20 percent federally, plus state taxes. Depreciation Recapture: Taxed at a maximum rate of 25 percent on the portion of the gain attributable to prior depreciation deductions.

These taxes can reduce your net profit substantially if not planned for. However, 1031 exchanges can defer these taxes indefinitely.

## Working with Tax Professionals

Given the complexity of real estate tax laws and the importance of proper planning, working with experienced tax professionals – CPAs or tax attorneys specializing in real estate – is essential.

They can: Help structure your investments for maximum tax efficiency. Assist with cost segregation studies, 1031 exchanges, and filing, and keep you informed of tax law changes affecting your investments.

Tax planning isn't a footnote – it's a profit driver.

By leveraging deductions, depreciation, 1031 exchanges, and advanced strategies like cost segregation, you can maximize your after-tax returns and accelerate wealth building. Understanding the tax implications of your investment decisions and working closely with professionals ensures that you keep more of your hard-earned profits while staying compliant with tax laws.

## Tax Strategies Checklist for Multifamily Investors

*Maximize Deductions*

- Track and document all operating expenses (repairs, maintenance, insurance, taxes).
- Keep detailed records of mortgage interest payments.
- Record professional fees related to the property

(legal, accounting, consulting).

- Track travel expenses related to property management activities.

### Leverage Depreciation

- Calculate annual depreciation for buildings and components.
- Consider a cost segregation study to accelerate depreciation deductions.
- Review depreciation schedules annually and adjust for improvements.

### Understand Passive Activity Rules

- Determine if you qualify for active participation to deduct rental losses.
- Evaluate if you or your spouse meet real estate professional status for full loss deductions.

### Plan for 1031 Exchanges

- Consult with a qualified intermediary and tax advisor before selling.
- Identify potential replacement properties within forty-five days after sale.
- Complete the purchase of the replacement property within 180 days to qualify.

### Explore Other Tax Incentives

- Research eligibility for Opportunity Zone investments or local tax credits.
- Monitor changes in tax laws that affect real estate investments.

### Prepare for Sale Taxes

- Calculate potential capital gains and depreciation recapture taxes before selling.
- Develop a plan to minimize tax liability (e.g., 1031 exchange, installment sale).

## *Engage Tax Professionals*

- Retain a CPA or tax attorney with real estate expertise.
- Schedule annual tax planning sessions to optimize strategies.
- Review tax returns carefully for accuracy and maximum deductions.

## Conclusion

The smartest investors don't just focus on finding deals; they focus on keeping more of what they earn. Taxes are one of the largest, yet most controllable, expenses in real estate investment. By approaching your strategy with foresight, surrounding yourself with the right advisors, and staying proactive about available incentives, you can transform your tax plan into a powerful tool for wealth creation. Let your tax plan do some of the heavy lifting.

Build your portfolio with intention and let your tax strategy become part of your edge.

## Reflection Questions

1. How well do you understand the tax deductions available to you as a multifamily investor?
2. Are you confident that you're capturing all eligible expenses to reduce taxable income?
3. Have you calculated your annual depreciation and considered cost segregation to accelerate deductions?
4. What steps can you take to implement or improve depreciation strategies?
5. Are you aware of the passive activity loss rules and how they might affect your ability to deduct losses?
6. Do you know whether you or your spouse qualify as real estate professionals?
7. Have you planned ahead for capital gains and depreciation recapture taxes when selling a prop-

erty?

8. What strategies can you use to defer or reduce these tax liabilities?

9. Do you have a process in place to evaluate the feasibility of 1031 exchanges before selling?

10. How comfortable are you with the timing and rules involved?

11. Are you utilizing tax professionals effectively to navigate complex real estate tax laws?

12. How often do you consult with your CPA or tax advisor about your investments?

13. Have you explored additional tax incentives, such as Opportunity Zones or local credits, that might apply to your properties?

14. How do your tax strategies align with your overall investment goals and timelines?

15. What is one tax planning improvement you can implement before your next tax filing?

16. How do you stay informed about changing tax laws that affect real estate investors?

# CHAPTER 11:
## RISK MANAGEMENT AND PROBLEM SOLVING – SAFEGUARDING YOUR MULTIFAMILY INVESTMENT

*"Risk comes from not knowing what you're doing."*
— Warren Buffett

Every investment carries risk, and multifamily real estate is no exception. While the potential rewards of stable cash flow and asset appreciation are enticing, they come with challenges that can impact your returns and peace of mind. Navigating tenant issues, vacancies, and market fluctuations requires more than just experience – it demands strong problem-solving skills and a well-defined strategy for managing risk.

This chapter introduces you to the key risks multifamily investors face and equips you with strategies to identify, mitigate, and manage them proactively.

## Identifying Common Risks in Multifamily Investing

Market Risk: Economic downturns, rising interest rates, or oversupply can reduce demand, lower rents, and depress property values.

Vacancy Risk: Prolonged vacancies reduce cash flow and can increase marketing and maintenance expenses.

Tenant Risk: Problematic tenants can cause late payments, property damage, or legal issues.

Maintenance and Repair Risk: Unexpected repairs or deferred maintenance can strain budgets.

Regulatory Risk: Changes in laws (rent control, eviction moratoriums, zoning) can affect operations and profitability.

Financial Risk: Interest rate increases, loan defaults, or cash flow shortages pose threats to your investment.

Natural Disasters and Environmental Risks: Floods, fires, or other disasters can cause property damage and liability concerns.

## Conducting Thorough Due Diligence

Risk management begins before acquisition:

Market Analysis: Assess local economic indicators, job growth, rental demand, and supply trends.

Property Inspection: Hire qualified inspectors to uncover hidden repair or compliance issues.

Financial Review: Scrutinize the seller's financials, rent rolls, and expense history.

Legal Review: Understand zoning, rent regulations, and any pending litigation.

Due diligence helps you spot red flags early and avoid risky deals or plan for contingencies.

## Mitigating Market and Vacancy Risks

Diversify Locations: Spread investments across different markets to reduce exposure to local downturns.

Set Realistic Rents: Price competitively based on market comps to minimize vacancy.

Enhance Tenant Retention: Invest in tenant relations, timely maintenance, and community-building to encourage lease renewals.

Create Financial Buffers: Maintain adequate reserves to cover vacancy periods and unexpected costs.

Managing Tenant Risks: Effectively managing tenant risk starts with thorough screening, clear and enforceable lease terms, and timely responses to concerns. This approach fosters respectful tenant relationships while safeguarding your property, preserving cash flow, and reducing turnover over the long term. Respond Promptly: Address tenant complaints and repair requests quickly to maintain goodwill. Document Everything: Keep detailed records of communications, payments, and incidents.

Controlling Maintenance and Unexpected Expenses requires a proactive approach through preventative maintenance, capital improvement planning, reliable vendor relationships, and diligent expense tracking to preserve property value and protect your bottom line.

Effectively Managing Property Expenses means implementing preventative maintenance, budgeting for capital improvements, partnering with trusted vendors, and closely monitoring costs to prevent unexpected breakdowns and financial overruns.

Navigating Regulatory and Legal Risks requires staying informed on changing laws, ensuring compliance through legal guidance, and actively engaging with industry groups to anticipate and adapt to evolving regulations that impact your multifamily investments.

Financial Risk Management involves aligning financing with your strategy, maintaining cash reserves, stress-testing for adverse scenarios, and monitoring debt ratios to ensure your multifamily investment remains resilient under pressure.

Preparing for Natural Disasters and Environmental Risks means creating emergency response plans and conducting risk assessments to protect your property, tenants, and investment from unexpected events.

A problem-solving mindset means staying proactive, communicating openly, seeking expert guidance, and remaining flexible – so you can spot challenges early, respond effectively, and continually improve your multifamily operations.

For example, when a spike in water bills revealed an undetected leak, instead of reacting with frustration, the property manager brought in a plumber, and I worked with the contractor to implement a long-term fix. We also installed water-saving devices in every unit. What started as a problem became an opportunity to cut costs and improve efficiency across the entire property.

## Conclusion

Risk is inherent in multifamily investing, but it doesn't have to derail your success. By identifying risks upfront, conducting thorough due diligence, and implementing thoughtful mitigation strategies, you can safeguard your investment and navigate challenges with confidence. Cultivating a problem-solving mindset ensures that when issues arise, you respond swiftly and effectively, turning potential setbacks into opportunities for growth. This is how resilient portfolios are built.

## Risk Management and Problem-Solving Checklist

### Risk Identification

- Review local market conditions and economic indicators regularly.
- Analyze vacancy trends and tenant turnover rates.
- Assess tenant profiles and screening processes.
- Inspect property condition and maintenance history.
- Stay updated on relevant landlord-tenant laws and regulations.
- Evaluate financing terms and debt service requirements.
- Identify environmental and natural disaster risks for your properties.

### Due Diligence

- Conduct thorough property inspections before acquisition.
- Verify the seller's financials, rent rolls, and oper-

ating expenses.

- Consult legal professionals on zoning and regulatory compliance.

### *Vacancy and Tenant Risk Mitigation*

- Set competitive rents based on market analysis.
- Implement rigorous tenant screening procedures.
- Develop tenant retention programs (maintenance responsiveness, community events).
- Maintain clear and enforceable lease agreements.

### *Maintenance and Expense Control*

- Establish a preventive maintenance schedule.
- Budget for capital improvements and unexpected repairs.
- Build relationships with trusted contractors and vendors.
- Monitor operating expenses monthly for variances.

### *Regulatory Compliance*

- Regularly review changes in local laws and fair housing regulations.
- Ensure leases and eviction procedures comply with legal standards.
- Train staff on compliance and tenant communication protocols.

### *Financial Risk Management*

- Maintain sufficient cash reserves for operating and capital expenses.
- Choose financing with terms suited to your investment strategy.
- Perform stress tests for worst-case scenarios (vacancy, rent reduction, interest rate hikes).
- Monitor loan-to-value and debt service coverage

ratios regularly.

### Disaster Preparedness

- Secure comprehensive insurance coverage (property, liability, hazard).
- Develop and communicate emergency response plans.
- Conduct regular safety inspections and hazard mitigation.

### Problem-Solving Practices

- Conduct periodic operational and financial reviews.
- Maintain open, proactive communication with tenants and staff.
- Consult with legal, financial, and property management professionals as needed.
- Document incidents, decisions, and resolutions thoroughly.

## Reflection Questions

1. What are the top three risks you currently face in your multifamily investment(s)?
2. How prepared are you to handle them?
3. How thorough was your due diligence process on your latest property acquisition?
4. What could you improve next time?
5. What strategies do you have in place to minimize vacancy and tenant-related risks?
6. How do you budget and plan for unexpected maintenance or capital expenditures?
7. Are you up to date with all relevant landlord-tenant laws and regulations affecting your properties?
8. How do you monitor your financial health, including cash reserves and debt ratios, to manage financial risks?
9. Do you have emergency or disaster preparedness

plans for your properties?

10. How often are they reviewed and updated?

11. How effective is your communication with tenants and property management teams when problems arise?

12. What professional resources (legal, financial, property management) do you rely on to solve issues?

13. What lessons have you learned from past challenges, and how have they shaped your current risk management approach?

# CHAPTER 12:
## BUILDING A STRONG BRAND AND EMBRACING SUSTAINABILITY – ATTRACTING TENANTS AND ENHANCING ASSET VALUE

*"Sustainability is no longer about doing less harm; it's about doing more good."*

— Jochen Zeitz

I'll never forget the moment my thinking about branding changed. I was touring one of our properties with a potential investor – someone I really wanted to impress. As we walked the grounds, he stopped and looked around. "It's clean," he said, "but what makes it yours?"

That question landed hard. Until then, I thought keeping the property well-maintained and cash-flowing was enough. But I realized I had overlooked something vital: the story we were telling, the identity we were projecting, the emotional impression we were making. We didn't have a brand – we just had a building.

That was the day I began to understand branding not as a logo or color scheme, but as the way people feel when they interact with your property, your team, and your mission. It's the experience, the reputation, the day-to-day feel of the place.

In this chapter, we'll explore how strategic branding helps your multifamily investment stand out in a crowded market. We'll cover how to define your brand, differentiate your properties, and align your messaging to attract not just tenants, but investors, partners, and community support.

Because a strong brand doesn't just fill units – it builds trust, increases retention, and elevates the perceived value of everything you touch.

In today's competitive multifamily market, attracting and retaining quality tenants goes far beyond just offering affordable rent and functional units. Savvy investors understand the power of building a strong brand that resonates with prospective renters and the community. At the same time, growing awareness and demand for sustainable, eco-friendly living presents a unique opportunity to differentiate your properties, reduce operating costs, and increase long-term value.

This chapter explores how combining strategic branding and marketing with sustainability initiatives creates a compelling value proposition that appeals to modern renters while boosting your investment's performance.

## The Power of a Strong Brand

A property's brand is much more than its name or logo – it's the emotional and practical experience you promise and deliver to tenants. A strong brand builds trust, fosters loyalty, and encourages word-of-mouth referrals, all of which drive occupancy and justify premium rents.

Define Your Brand Identity: Consider what makes your property unique. Is it the location, amenities, community vibe, or commitment to sustainability? Develop a consistent message and visual identity that reflects these strengths.

Tell Your Story: Use your marketing channels – website, social media, advertising – to tell a compelling story about your property. Highlight what tenants value, whether it's walkability, safety, lifestyle, or green features.

Create a Tenant-Centric Experience: Brand promises must translate into day-to-day tenant interactions. Responsive management, well-maintained facilities, and community-building events reinforce your brand's credibility.

## Brand Example: The Cardone 10X Power

Grant Cardone built one of the most recognizable brands in multifamily real estate. His "10X" mantra isn't just a tagline – it's woven into every aspect of his properties, capital strategy, and public presence. With over $4 to 5 billion in multifamily assets under management, Cardone lives his brand every day.

- **Logo and visuals: Bold, black-and-white simplicity echoes power and clarity.**
- **Messaging: His promise – "10X your income, business, and life" – is repeated in every investor pitch, property brochure, and social media post.**
- **Positioning: He chose large, high-density multifamily buildings intentionally, reinforcing his "think big" philosophy.**

Why it works:

1. **Clarity – Investors know exactly what they're getting: aggressive growth, bold ambition, and high performance.**
2. **Consistency – From signage to syndication decks, the brand is unmistakably 10X.**
3. **Trust – The personality behind the brand reinforces credibility – investors follow not just the deals, but the vision.**
4. **You don't need "10X" to succeed – but the lesson is universal: your brand is not an afterthought; it's a strategic asset. It shapes how tenants feel, how brokers respond, and how investors perceive your leadership. By treating your brand as an extension of your strategy, you elevate your properties from "just buildings" to experiences that resonate, retain, and command premium value.**

Digital marketing is a cornerstone of modern tenant acquisition. Strategies like building a professional, mobile-friendly website, engaging on social media, managing online reviews, and running targeted ads all work together to showcase your property's value, build trust, and attract the right renters efficiently.

Community Engagement and Tenant Retention means organizing tenant events (e.g., BBQs, fitness classes, sustainability workshops) that foster connection and pride. Communication Channels maintain open and friendly communication via newsletters, social media groups, or the community. Prompt maintenance and management responses boost tenant satisfaction and brand reputation.

Sustainability as a competitive advantage means meeting growing tenant and investor demand by integrating energy efficiency, water conservation, waste reduction, and healthy indoor environments – boosting property value, lowering operating costs, and setting your multifamily asset apart in a crowded market.

Green Certifications and Marketing require obtaining certifications such as LEED, ENERGY STAR, or Green Globes signals your commitment to sustainability and can be a powerful marketing tool. Certified properties often command higher rents, attract quality tenants, and may qualify for tax incentives or rebates.

The financial benefits of sustainability go beyond tenant appeal by lowering energy and water costs, reducing maintenance through durable materials, boosting property value, and unlocking incentives like grants, tax credits, and favorable financing – all of which enhance net operating income and long-term returns.

Integrating branding and sustainability creates a powerful, differentiated tenant experience by showcasing green initiatives in marketing, making sustainability a core brand value, involving residents in eco-friendly practices, and sharing measurable impact to foster loyalty and community pride.

For example, I helped reposition a mid-century apartment complex by upgrading units with energy-efficient appliances, installing solar panels, and launching community recycling programs. We rebranded the property as a "green urban oasis," leveraging social media and local events to highlight these features. Result: occupancy rose from 85 percent to 98 percent, rents increased by 12 percent, and operating expenses dropped by 15 percent, boosting overall asset value and tenant satisfaction.

Building a strong brand while embracing sustainability is a powerful strategy for multifamily investors seeking to attract quality tenants, enhance retention, reduce costs, and increase asset value. By integrating marketing, community engagement, and green initiatives, you create a compelling offer that resonates with today's renters and positions your investment for long-term success.

## Branding and Sustainability Checklist for Multifamily Investors

### *Building a Strong Brand*

- Define your property's unique value proposition and brand identity.
- Develop consistent messaging and visual elements across all marketing channels.
- Create a professional, mobile-friendly website with high-quality photos and virtual tours.
- Engage regularly on social media platforms relevant to your target tenants.
- Collect and manage online tenant reviews; respond professionally to feedback.
- Implement targeted digital advertising campaigns to reach ideal tenant demographics.
- Organize tenant-focused community events and activities to build engagement.
- Maintain prompt, transparent communication channels with tenants.

### *Integrating Sustainability*

- Conduct an energy audit to identify opportunities for efficiency upgrades.
- Install energy-efficient lighting, appliances, and smart thermostats.
- Implement water-saving fixtures and drought-resistant landscaping.
- Establish waste reduction programs, including recycling and composting.
- Use low-VOC paints and materials to improve indoor air quality.
- Pursue green building certifications (e.g., LEED, ENERGY STAR) if applicable.
- Educate tenants on sustainability initiatives and encourage participation.
- Monitor and track sustainability metrics (energy savings, water use, waste reduction).

### *Financial and Operational Benefits*

- Analyze cost savings from energy and water efficiency improvements.
- Apply for available grants, rebates, or tax incentives for sustainable upgrades.
- Evaluate the impact of sustainability on property valuation and tenant demand.

## Conclusion

Reflect on the example of the 10X brand built by Grant Cardone. He turned bold messaging, visual consistency, and relentless clarity into a multifamily powerhouse with billions in assets under management. His brand isn't just about style – it's a strategy that attracts investors, inspires tenants, and drives growth. That's the power of branding done right.

You don't need a global stage to build a great brand. You just need intention. What you stand for, how you show up, and what you consistently deliver – that's your brand. So, define it, own it, and let it guide every interaction with your properties and your people. Because in a sea of sameness, the right brand is your unfair advantage. A strong brand backed by real values doesn't just fill units – it builds lasting relationships.

## Reflection Questions

- What unique qualities or values define your property's brand?
- How clearly and consistently are these communicated to prospective tenants?
- How effective is your current digital marketing strategy in reaching and engaging quality tenants?
- What are your current strengths and weaknesses in tenant community engagement?
- How could you enhance tenant loyalty and satisfaction?
- Have you evaluated your property's energy and water efficiency?
- What sustainability upgrades could provide the best return on investment?
- Are you actively promoting your sustainability initiatives as part of your property's brand?
- How do you measure and communicate the impact of your green investments to tenants and stakeholders?
- What barriers, if any, have you encountered in implementing sustainability measures?
- How might you overcome them?
- How do your branding and sustainability efforts align with your overall investment goals and tenant demographics?

- Have you explored green certifications or local incentives that could enhance your property's marketability and financial performance?
- What is one immediate action you can take to strengthen your property's brand or sustainability profile?

# CHAPTER 13:
## MANAGING PROFIT AND PERFORMANCE

*"The property you buy sets the stage, but how you manage it writes the story of your success."*
— Maria L. Ellis

Buying a property is an achievement – but managing it well is where real profits are made. Without a strategy, ownership brings stress. With systems, it builds stability, cash flow, and long-term value.

The truth is, your returns don't just come from the deal you buy; they come from how well you operate it every day after.

In this chapter, we'll look at how to manage your multi-family properties like a business. From optimizing rents and creating maintenance schedules to selecting the right tech tools and tracking performance, you'll learn how to maximize income, protect your assets, and ensure your investments thrive year after year.

Buying a property is only the beginning. Owning it well – day in and day out – is what separates great investors from good ones.

Many first-time investors focus on the deal itself: the purchase price, financing, and closing. But once the ink dries, the real work begins. Managing your asset effectively determines whether it becomes a cash-flowing machine or a constant source of stress.

In this chapter, we'll look at how to run your property like a business – from maximizing revenue and minimizing expenses to maintaining tenant satisfaction and preserving long-term value. Whether you manage or hire professionals, these are the skills and systems that keep your investment strong.

## Asset Management versus Property Management

Property management is about the day-to-day: leasing, rent collection, maintenance, and tenant relations. Asset management is about the bigger picture: financial performance, budgeting, capital improvements, and long-term strategy. Even if you outsource property management, taking full ownership of the asset management role is what separates passive landlords from intentional investors.

You're the CEO of your investment. The manager works in the business. You work on the business.

## Rent Optimization Strategies

Your property's income is directly tied to how well you manage pricing and occupancy.

To optimize rent:

Know your comps. Regularly review what similar units are rented for in your area. Incentivize renewals. Offer minor upgrades or flexible terms for good tenants. Implement annual increases. Even modest increases protect you from inflation and rising costs. Use tiered pricing. Charge premiums for upgrades (e.g., renovated units, corner layouts, better views).

Leverage tools like Rentometer, Zillow Rental Manager, or revenue management platforms to help analyze pricing.

Rentometer streamlines rent-comparative market analysis by allowing landlords and investors to instantly generate local rental comps, refine data with adjustable filters, scale insights across multiple properties, and create professional, branded reports – making rent pricing faster, more accurate, and more credible.

Zillow Rental Manager is a comprehensive platform

that helps landlords streamline rental operations by offering wide listing exposure, free tenant screening, digital leasing, and online rent collection – all in one centralized, easy-to-use dashboard that saves time, increases visibility, and enhances professionalism.

Revenue management platforms help analyze and optimize rental pricing by using real-time market data, historical trends, and occupancy patterns to maximize income and maintain competitive positioning.

Maintenance: Proactive Beats Reactive – because deferring maintenance damages cash flow and tenant satisfaction, it is essential to follow a regular inspection schedule, fund capital reserves, and treat maintenance like insurance that safeguards your property's long-term value and performance. Deferred maintenance is a cash-flow killer – and a tenant satisfaction risk. Keep a capex reserve fund – typically $250 to $300 per unit annually – to cover larger expenses like roof repairs, appliance replacement, or parking lot resurfacing. Treat maintenance like insurance – it protects everything you've built.

Tenant retention is cash flow preservation as minimizing turnover through responsive maintenance, clear communication, small renewal incentives, and community-building efforts reduces vacancy costs, boosts tenant satisfaction, and protects your bottom line. Vacancies cost time and money – marketing, cleaning, lost rent, and re-tenanting stress.

Property management options – whether self-managing, hiring a professional, or using hybrid platforms– should align with your goals and capacity, but regardless of the approach, staying engaged through regular oversight and communication is essential to protect your investment. Whichever you choose, stay involved. Review reports, inspect properties periodically, and maintain communication with tenants and vendors.

## Tech Tools That Make You More Efficient

Technology can simplify every aspect of property management and improve performance:

### Rent Collection and Financials

Buildium: A comprehensive property management software that offers rent collection, accounting, and financial reporting tools designed for small to mid-sized multifamily portfolios. It streamlines tenant payments and automates financial tracking.

AppFolio: A robust cloud-based platform providing rent collection, expense management, and detailed financial reporting. It supports online payments and offers integrated accounting features, suitable for growing property management businesses.

RentRedi: Focused on simplifying rent collection and tenant communication, RentRedi offers easy-to-use online payment processing and financial tracking tools. It's well-suited for landlords managing smaller portfolios or single-family rentals.

Stessa: A free, user-friendly financial tracking platform tailored for real estate investors. Stessa automates income and expense tracking, rent collection monitoring, and provides insightful performance dashboards, making it ideal for investors wanting cost-effective financial oversight.

### Tenant Communication and Leasing

TenantCloud: A cloud-based platform offering tenant communication, online rental applications, lease management, and maintenance request tracking. It facilitates seamless interaction between landlords and tenants and supports online payments.

Hemlane: Designed for remote landlords, Hemlane provides tenant screening, lease management, rent collection, and communication tools. It offers a centralized platform to manage leasing activities and tenant relationships efficiently from anywhere.

TurboTenant: A user-friendly tool focused on marketing rental properties, tenant screening, and online applications. TurboTenant helps landlords attract tenants and manage leasing documents with ease, streamlining the tenant onboarding process.

Cozy: An integrated platform that combines online leasing, tenant screening, and rent collection. Cozy simplifies the rental process by providing landlords with tools to manage leases, vet applicants, and collect rent all in one place.

### Maintenance and Operations

Property Meld: An automated maintenance tracking platform designed to streamline work order management. It facilitates communication between property managers, tenants, and vendors, helping to prioritize, assign, and track maintenance requests efficiently.

Trello or Asana: Popular task and project management tools that can be adapted for property maintenance and vendor coordination. They allow you to organize tasks, set deadlines, assign responsibilities, and monitor progress through customizable boards or lists.

Google Drive or Notion: Cloud-based platforms ideal for storing important documents such as Standard Operating Procedures (SOPs), vendor contacts, and property information. Both offer collaborative features that enable teams to access and update information in real-time.

### Performance Dashboards

DealCheck: A real estate analysis platform focused on tracking cash flow, return on investment (ROI), and key deal metrics. It helps investors evaluate and monitor property performance with easy-to-understand dashboards and scenario modeling.

QuickBooks or Xero: Robust accounting software widely used by real estate investors and businesses. Both platforms offer comprehensive bookkeeping, expense tracking, financial reporting, and integration capabilities tailored to real estate entities, enabling accurate and organized financial management.

Use tools that integrate well and reduce time spent on

repetitive tasks – so you can focus on strategy, not paperwork.

## Monthly and Quarterly Asset Management Review

Set recurring checkpoints to evaluate your property's performance:

### *Monthly*

Here's a summary of key monthly property management metrics:

Rent Collection versus Expected Income: Tracking actual rent payments received compared to projected rental income to monitor cash flow health and identify delinquencies early.

Expense Review: Analyzing monthly operating expenses to ensure spending aligns with budgets and to detect any unusual or excessive costs.

Maintenance Ticket Status: Reviewing the progress and resolution of maintenance requests to ensure timely repairs and tenant satisfaction.

Vacancy and Turnover Updates: Monitoring current vacancy rates and tenant turnover activity to assess occupancy trends and plan leasing efforts.

To organize and report your monthly property management metrics effectively, consider these tips:

Create a Monthly Dashboard: Use a spreadsheet or property management software to compile key metrics – rent collected, expenses, maintenance status, and vacancy rates – into a clear, visual dashboard with charts and tables for quick insights.

Set Benchmarks: Establish target goals for each metric (e.g., 98 percent rent collection rate, expenses within budget, maintenance requests closed within seven days, vacancy below 5 percent) to easily identify areas needing attention.

Use Color Coding: Highlight metrics that are on track in green, borderline in yellow, and problematic in red to draw focus to issues needing action.

Include Narrative Summaries: Accompany data with brief notes explaining significant variances, upcoming challenges, or completed improvements for context.

Automate Data Collection: Integrate accounting, maintenance, and leasing platforms where possible to pull data automatically and reduce errors.

Distribute Reports to Stakeholders: Share monthly reports with owners, property managers, and investors to maintain transparency and facilitate timely decisions.

Review Trends Over Time: Compare current month data to previous months and the same period last year to identify patterns or seasonal fluctuations.

### Quarterly

Here's a summary of key quarterly property management activities:

Rent Comparables and Potential Increases: Review local market rents to assess opportunities for rent adjustments and ensure your pricing remains competitive.

Capital Expense Planning: Evaluate upcoming major repairs or improvements, budgeting for capital expenditures to maintain and enhance property value.

Property Walk-Through or Virtual Inspection: Conduct thorough inspections to identify maintenance needs, safety issues, and opportunities for upgrades.

Update Your Pro Forma versus Actuals: Compare your financial projections with actual performance to assess accuracy, identify variances, and adjust strategies accordingly.

This quarterly rhythm helps you monitor trends, make informed decisions, and safeguard your property's profitability over time.

## Managing for the Long Run

The best investors plan like portfolio managers, not house flippers. They think in decades, not months. They know that real estate success comes not just from buying well – but from managing with care, consistency, and vision.

## Conclusion

Real estate wealth is built through consistent, intentional management. When you operate with clear systems, proactive maintenance, and a focus on tenant satisfaction, you don't just preserve your property – you enhance its value and performance. Whether you self-manage or delegate to professionals, staying engaged as an asset manager ensures your investment delivers on its full potential. In the next chapter, we'll explore the art of raising capital – the essential skill that allows you to grow beyond your personal funds and bring others along with you on the journey toward wealth and impact.

## Managing Profit and Performance Checklist

### *Financial Management*

- Monitor monthly rent collection and compare it against expected income.
- Regularly review operating expenses to identify savings opportunities.
- Analyze net operating income (NOI) and cash flow trends.
- Track key financial metrics such as cap rate, debt service coverage ratio (DSCR), and return on investment (ROI).

### *Rent Optimization*

- Conduct regular market rent analysis to ensure competitive pricing.
- Adjust rents strategically based on vacancy rates, lease expirations, and market conditions.
- Implement tenant retention programs to reduce turnover and vacancy costs.

### *Maintenance and Repairs*

- Establish a preventive maintenance schedule to avoid costly emergency repairs.

- Monitor and prioritize maintenance requests for timely resolution.
- Manage vendor relationships to ensure quality work and competitive pricing.

### *Technology and Property Management Tools*

- Utilize property management software to automate rent collection, communication, and reporting.
- Implement maintenance tracking platforms to streamline work orders and vendor management.
- Leverage financial dashboards for real-time performance monitoring.

### *Staff and Vendor Management*

- Train property management staff on operational best practices and customer service.
- Set clear performance expectations and regularly review staff performance.
- Negotiate contracts and terms with vendors to maximize value.

### *Compliance and Risk Management*

- Ensure ongoing compliance with local landlord-tenant laws and building codes.
- Maintain appropriate insurance coverage and safety protocols.
- Conduct regular property inspections to identify and mitigate risks.

## Reflection Questions

1. How do you currently manage your rental properties (self-managed, third-party, hybrid)?
2. Is this approach serving your time, financial, and lifestyle goals?
3. Do you have a clear distinction between property management and asset management in your real estate business?

4. If not, how can you begin to step more fully into the asset manager role?
5. When was the last time you reviewed your rent rates compared to the market?
6. Could your units be priced more effectively based on amenities or comps?
7. Do you have a preventive maintenance schedule in place?
8. What recurring tasks can you implement to protect your investment and reduce emergency repairs?
9. What systems do you use to track property income, expenses, and tenant communications?
10. Are there tech tools that could streamline your operations?
11. How would you rate your tenant retention strategy?
12. What's one improvement you could make to increase tenant satisfaction and renewals?
13. Do you set aside capital reserves for repairs and upgrades?
14. If not, how much should you begin saving annually per unit to plan responsibly?
15. How frequently do you review your property's financial performance?
16. Could you benefit from implementing monthly or quarterly review check-ins?
17. Which tech platforms mentioned in this chapter could support your current or future property management strategy?
18. Make a list of one to two to explore this month.
19. What is one change you can implement this week to improve the management, efficiency, or profitability of a current property?

# CHAPTER 14:
# RAISING CAPITAL WITH INTEGRITY

*"Trust is earned in drops and lost in buckets."*
— Kevin Plank

At some point in your real estate journey, you'll reach the limit of your capital – and that's a good thing. It means you're ready to grow. Once you hit your own capital ceiling, the next step isn't taking on more risk – it's learning to raise money with transparency, structure, and trust.

In this chapter, we'll explore how to attract investors, structure partnerships, and raise funds ethically and legally. Whether you're partnering with friends, working with accredited investors, or launching your first syndication, you'll learn how to position your deals as opportunities – not asks – and how to become a trusted steward of someone else's capital with the highest level of integrity.

Real estate is one of the most powerful vehicles for building wealth – but it's also capital-intensive. Sooner or later, every investor reaches a point where their personal funds aren't enough to seize the right opportunities. The good news is: you don't need to fund every deal yourself.

Most large-scale investors grow by raising capital from people who want real estate returns – without doing the work themselves.

But raising capital is about more than just money. It's about trust. And trust is built on integrity, transparency, and the ability to deliver results.

In this chapter, I'll show you how to approach capital raising the right way – ethically, legally, and strategically – so you can grow your business while helping others achieve their financial goals.

## Who Should Raise Capital?

You don't need to be wealthy, famous, or have decades of experience to raise capital. What you *do* need is:

- A solid understanding of your market and deal type
- A clear investment strategy and track record (or a credible team)
- The ability to communicate confidently and transparently
- A deep respect for other people's money

If you're serious about treating your investors like partners and protecting their interests, you're on the right path.

## Understanding Securities Laws (and Why They Matter)

The moment you accept someone else's money, especially in a passive role, you step into the world of securities law. Even if you're not selling stock, you may be offering a "security," which is regulated by the SEC.

Here are two common legal structures for raising capital:

### *Joint Ventures (JVs)*

- Two or more people pool resources and actively participate in managing the deal.
- Ideal for small projects or partnerships with equal roles.

### *Syndications*

- One person or team (the "General Partner" or GP) manages the deal.
- Others (the "Limited Partners" or LPs) invest

capital passively and receive returns.

- Must comply with securities regulations – usually under exemptions like Regulation D (506(b) or 506(c)).

Always consult a real estate attorney experienced in syndications before raising capital or pooling investor funds. The penalties for non-compliance are serious.

## The Mindset of a Capital Raiser

When you raise money, you are not asking for a favor – you are offering an opportunity.

You're giving people a chance to:

- Diversify their portfolio
- Gain access to deals they couldn't find or manage alone
- Earn passive income, tax benefits, and long-term appreciation
- Be clear, honest, and realistic – not salesy or aggressive. This is a long game.

## How to Build Trust with Investors

1. Start with people you know
   - Colleagues, family, business contacts
   - Let them know what you're doing and how they can learn more
2. Educate before you ask
   - Share insights, case studies, and sample deals
   - Host webinars or coffee chats
3. Create a simple investor packet
   - Executive summary of the deal
   - Investment terms and structure
   - Market overview
   - Risk disclosure
4. Be honest about risk
   - Real estate is not risk-free. Be transparent.

  o Share how you mitigate risk and what contingencies you have in place.
5. Deliver consistent communication
  o Before, during, and after the deal
  o Use updates, financial reports, and investor calls to maintain trust

## Example: From Relationship to Raise

One of my early investors was a former banking colleague who had capital but no time to manage properties. I wasn't just offering a return; I was offering peace of mind, transparency, and a chance to grow his wealth alongside mine.

Our existing trust and my clear strategy made the conversation natural. That first investment opened the door to more – because delivering results builds credibility.

## Common Mistakes to Avoid

  o **Overpromising returns – Always use conservative estimates**
  o **Underestimating expenses – Protect your investors by being realistic**
  o **Poor communication – Silence creates fear; keep investors informed**
  o **Legal shortcuts – Never raise capital without the right legal structure – it's not just risky; it's illegal.**

## Growing with Integrity

Raising capital is a responsibility. When someone invests with you, they're entrusting you with their hard-earned money, their goals, and their future. That trust is sacred. Protecting it should be your highest priority.

## Conclusion

Your reputation is your most valuable asset. Build it one deal, one investor, one promise kept at a time. Raising capital is not just about funding deals – it's about building relationships rooted in trust, transparency, and shared success. When you approach investors with integrity, deliver consistent results, and communicate openly, you become more than a dealmaker; you become a trusted partner. As your network grows, so does your ability to scale, diversify, and make a meaningful impact.

## Raising Capital with Integrity Checklist

### *Preparation and Planning*

- Clearly define your investment opportunity and value proposition.
- Prepare comprehensive, transparent offering materials (pitch decks, financial projections, risk disclosures).
- Understand applicable securities laws and regulations to ensure compliance.

### *Building Trust with Investors*

- Communicate openly and honestly about risks and potential returns.
- Provide timely and accurate updates throughout the investment lifecycle.
- Establish clear expectations regarding investor involvement and reporting.

### *Sourcing and Screening Investors*

- Identify investors whose goals and risk tolerance align with your offering.
- Conduct due diligence on prospective investors as appropriate.
- Build relationships based on mutual respect and shared objectives.

### *Legal and Ethical Compliance*

- Work with qualified legal counsel to draft and review all offering documents.
- Ensure all marketing and communication materials are truthful and not misleading.

- Adhere strictly to disclosure requirements and anti-fraud provisions.

### Managing Investor Relations

- Maintain organized records of investor communications and agreements.
- Respond promptly to investor inquiries and concerns.
- Facilitate transparent distribution of financial reports and returns.

### Continuous Improvement

- Solicit feedback from investors to improve processes and communications.
- Stay informed on changes in securities regulations and best practices.
- Commit to ongoing education on ethical capital raising and investor relations.

## Reflection Questions

1. Have you ever raised capital or managed someone else's money before?
2. If so, what did you learn from the experience? If not, what excites or intimidates you about it?
3. Who in your personal or professional network might be interested in passive real estate investment? List three to five people you could start a conversation with.
4. What kind of opportunity would you feel comfortable offering to others?
5. (e.g., joint venture, small multifamily, value-add project, long-term hold)
6. Do you understand the legal requirements for raising capital in your state or country?
7. Have you spoken with a real estate attorney about forming a syndication or joint venture?
8. How will you present opportunities to potential investors?

9. (Investor packet, slide deck, email summary, in-person meetings?) What materials do you need to create?
10. How confident are you in explaining both the risks and rewards of an investment?
11. If you're not yet confident, what can you do to strengthen your knowledge and communication?
12. What systems or habits can you put in place to keep investors informed and engaged throughout a deal?
13. What is your plan for protecting your investors' capital, and how will you communicate that plan clearly?
14. What values do you want to be known for as a capital raiser?
15. (e.g., transparency, integrity, reliability, expertise)
16. What is one action step you can take this week to move closer to raising capital responsibly and confidently?

# CHAPTER 15:
# SCALING YOUR PORTFOLIO
# – STRATEGIES FOR GROWTH
# WITHOUT BURNOUT

*"Scaling is not about doing everything –*
*it's about doing the right things with the right people*
*so you can grow without burning out."*
— Maria L. Ellis

The key to sustainable growth lies in working smarter – not just harder. This chapter focuses on practical strategies to scale your investments efficiently, maximize your leverage, and build a team that supports your expanding vision.

Let me share the story of how I learned this firsthand. When I acquired my first twelve-unit multifamily property, I did almost everything myself. I found the deal, walked the units, negotiated the loan, met the tenants, and even coordinated minor repairs. It felt empowering at first – but I was quickly stretched thin. When I purchased a second property just a year later, the demands doubled, but my capacity didn't.

That's when I realized that continuing to grow without a system – or a team – was a recipe for exhaustion.

I began by hiring a property management company and delegating routine operations. Then, I brought in a virtual assistant to help with investor communications and admin tasks. As I scaled to more than 100 units, I leaned on a reliable acquisitions partner to help evaluate new deals and a construction manager to oversee renovations. Each new team member gave me more clarity, more breathing room, and the capacity to think beyond daily fires.

Most importantly, it allowed me to focus on vision and strategy instead of getting stuck in the weeds.

Scaling isn't just about stacking properties – it's about designing a business that works for you – not one that runs you into the ground. In the pages ahead, we'll explore how to grow your portfolio using systems, partnerships, technology, and a mindset that prioritizes sustainability over speed.

Because long-term success isn't about doing more – it's about building smarter.

Growing from owning a single multifamily property to managing a robust portfolio is the aspiration of many investors. Yet, scaling brings its own unique challenges, complexities, increased responsibilities, and potential burnout. The key to sustainable growth lies in working smarter, not harder. This chapter focuses on practical strategies to scale your investments efficiently, maximize your leverage, and build a team that supports your expanding vision.

## Systematize Your Operations

Systematizing your operations is a foundational pillar for sustainable scaling. As your portfolio expands, managing each property ad hoc – as you might have with your first investment – quickly becomes unmanageable. That's why developing standardized processes is critical. Create detailed SOPs (Standard Operating Procedures), checklists, and templates for everything from tenant onboarding and rent collection to maintenance requests and financial reporting. Implement property management software that automates reminders, tracks maintenance, and consolidates communications. And most importantly, document everything in a way that's clear and accessible to your team. These systems reduce human error, save valuable time, and enable consistency across properties – giving you the structure to scale without chaos. As you acquire more properties, managing each one the same way you managed your first becomes impractical. Systematization is essential.

## Leverage Strategic Partnerships

Equally vital to your growth strategy is the ability to form and leverage strategic partnerships. No investor succeeds alone – especially when the scale and complexity of deals increase. Joint ventures (JVs) offer the opportunity to collaborate with other investors, pooling capital, sharing risk, and combining expertise to tackle projects that may be out of reach individually. Syndications allow you to act as a sponsor or invest as a limited partner, giving you access to larger, more lucrative deals. Beyond capital partners, surround yourself with professional service providers who understand your goals – brokers who know your criteria, attorneys who specialize in multifamily transactions, lenders who provide flexible financing, and accountants who ensure you're optimizing your tax position. The right partners extend your capabilities, de-risk your investments, and empower you to scale faster, smarter, and with greater confidence.

## Master Refinancing and Equity Recycling

Mastering refinancing and learning how to reuse your equity strategically is essential for investors looking to grow aggressively without relying solely on fresh capital. By tapping into the increased value of stabilized properties, you can unlock equity through cash-out refinancing and redeploy that capital into new deals. Timing is everything – monitor market conditions, property appreciation, and interest rates to determine when refinancing makes the most financial sense. Strategic use of tools like 1031 exchanges allows you to sell appreciated properties, defer capital gains taxes, and reinvest in higher-yield opportunities without eroding your returns. By recycling equity in this way, you're not only multiplying your buying power but also creating a repeatable process for sustainable, tax-efficient portfolio expansion.

## Build and Scale Your Team

To keep pace with growth, building and scaling your team becomes essential. Your team is your greatest force multiplier – enabling you to manage complexity without being overwhelmed. Hire experienced property managers to offload daily operations and free yourself to focus on strategy. Add support roles such as leasing agents, maintenance coordinators, bookkeepers, and acquisition analysts to strengthen all sides of your operation. Invest in your team's leadership potential by offering training and development that prepares them to step into more advanced roles as your business scales. And use collaboration tools and project management software to keep everyone connected and aligned, even across multiple properties. A well-coordinated, empowered team doesn't just support growth – it makes it possible.

## Focus on Continuous Learning and Adaptation

Scaling your multifamily portfolio is not just about stacking doors – adding units to your portfolio – but about evolving your skill set and sharpening your mindset. Committing to continuous learning means staying active in your education by attending industry seminars, workshops, and mastermind groups that focus specifically on scaling strategies. These environments not only provide fresh ideas but also expose you to peers who are tackling similar challenges. Just as important is analyzing the performance of your portfolio. Make it a habit to review key metrics regularly and adjust your strategy based on what the data is telling you. Market conditions, lending terms, tenant demographics, and technologies are always shifting. By staying informed and flexible, you'll build a business that's agile, relevant, and positioned for long-term success.

## Scaling Your Portfolio Checklist

### *Systematize Operations*

Systematizing operations is a cornerstone of sustainable scaling. Begin by documenting Standard Operating Procedures (SOPs) for all recurring and critical activities – things like rent collection, tenant screening, and maintenance workflows. These written processes provide consistency across your portfolio and reduce the reliance on any one individual's memory or habits. Use property management software to automate routine tasks, reduce errors, and free up time across your portfolio, ensuring routine tasks are handled efficiently and errors are minimized. Additionally, creating templates for financial reports, lease agreements, and tenant communications saves time and reinforces professionalism at every touchpoint. When operations are standardized and supported by smart tools, your growing portfolio becomes easier to manage – and much more resilient.

### *Leverage Partners and Teams*

An important key to scaling efficiently is leveraging strong partnerships and well-structured teams. As your portfolio grows, the day-to-day operational load becomes too much for any one person to manage effectively. That's why it's vital to build a reliable team that includes experienced property managers, leasing agents, and maintenance professionals – people you can trust to handle responsibilities without constant oversight. Clearly defined roles prevent confusion and empower each team member to make informed decisions within their area of expertise. Keep everyone aligned through regular updates, simple reporting habits, and open lines of feedback. When you invest in strong partnerships and create a culture of trust and communication, your business becomes more scalable, more stable, and better prepared for continued growth.

### *Refinance Strategically*

Strategic refinancing is another powerful tool for unlocking capital and fueling continued growth. Begin by monitoring your loan terms, including mortgage maturities and interest rate trends, so you can identify optimal moments to refinance. When done at the right time, refinancing allows you to pull out equity from an appreciated property and reinvest it into new acquisitions or property improvements. However, it's critical to weigh the costs versus the benefits – closing costs, prepayment penalties, and any changes in monthly cash flow should all be part of your analysis. When timed right, refinancing doesn't just strengthen your position – it keeps your momentum alive.

Let me share a story that illustrates just how powerful refinancing can be. A few years ago, one of my clients acquired a seventy-two-unit property in an emerging market. We executed a value-add strategy – renovated units, improved amenities, and raised rents. Within eighteen months, the property's value had significantly increased. Rather than hold tight, I helped my client refinance the property. By doing so, we were able to pull out a substantial portion of the equity while still maintaining positive cash flow. That capital was then rolled directly into the down payment on another asset – this time a ninety-six-unit property that I wouldn't have been able to purchase otherwise. One smart refinance created the financial leverage to double our portfolio size without taking on unnecessary risk or overleveraging. It's a prime example of how refinancing, when timed right and backed by strong fundamentals, becomes more than a financial tool – it becomes a growth accelerator.

### Scale Your Team Efficiently

As your portfolio expands, it becomes essential to scale your team with just as much strategy as your assets. Hire for where you're going, not just where you are. Look for people whose skills match the next stage of your business – bring in professionals whose skills align with the next level of your operations. Whether it's asset managers, construction leads, or acquisitions analysts, choose people who complement your vision and fill existing gaps. Once they're on board, provide consistent training and professional development so your team evolves alongside your growth. Technology also plays a critical role – use project management and communication tools to coordinate workflows, enhance accountability, and maintain clarity as your team grows. A well-built, well-managed team is your most valuable scaling engine.

### *Continuous Learning and Adaptation*

Finally, the most successful investors commit to continuous learning and adaptation. The multifamily landscape is dynamic – markets shift, regulations evolve, and technology advances. Staying ahead means staying informed. Attend industry seminars, workshops, and networking events that focus on multifamily scaling. These environments are rich with insights, case studies, and connections that can sharpen your strategy. Regularly review your portfolio's performance metrics and be willing to pivot when needed. Whether it's adjusting your underwriting assumptions, shifting markets, or integrating new systems, adaptability is key. Treat each property, each deal, and each lesson as a building block toward a more informed, resilient investment approach.

## Scaling Your Portfolio – Strategies for Growth Without Burnout Checklist

### *Systematize Operations*

To keep scaling on solid footing, it's also essential to systematize your operations. Begin by documenting standard operating procedures (SOPs) for every key function – rent collection, tenant screening, maintenance requests, and more. Clear SOPs ensure consistency, reduce errors, and make onboarding new team members more efficient. Implement property management software to automate routine tasks and centralize communication. Additionally, use templates for financial reporting and tenant correspondence to maintain professional, timely interactions.

These systems free up your time, enhance reliability, and make your business easier to manage at scale.

### Build and Leverage Your Team

Scaling also requires building and leveraging the right team around you. Start by identifying the key roles that will support your expanding operations – property managers to handle day-to-day logistics, leasing agents to maintain high occupancy, and maintenance staff to ensure the asset remains in peak condition. Delegating these responsibilities clearly ensures everyone knows their role, prevents micromanagement, and allows you to operate at a higher strategic level. But it's not enough to just fill positions – you need to invest in the growth of your team. Providing training, mentorship, and development opportunities strengthens their performance and deepens their commitment to your shared vision. A strong, well-supported team multiplies your capacity and makes scaling not only possible but sustainable for the long haul.

### Financial Planning and Management

Financial planning is an essential pillar of portfolio growth. Monitoring your cash flow closely helps ensure that you can support day-to-day operations and reinvest in your portfolio without overextending yourself. Strategic refinancing can also be a powerful tool – done at the right time, it can unlock trapped equity and free up capital for new acquisitions or renovations. But with every expansion comes greater risk, which is why maintaining adequate reserves is critical. Unexpected vacancies, repairs, or economic downturns can strain your finances, and having a financial cushion ensures you can navigate challenges without compromising your long-term goals. When your financial planning is proactive and precise, growth becomes not only possible – but sustainable.

### Leverage Technology

Another powerful lever for sustainable growth is technology. Leveraging integrated platforms for property management, accounting, and communication can dramatically increase efficiency and reduce manual errors. Tools that automate rent collection, maintenance tracking, and investor reporting free up your time and allow you to focus on strategy instead of spreadsheets. With the right systems in place, you can monitor performance across your portfolio in real time, make data-informed decisions faster, and stay ahead of operational challenges. Technology isn't just a convenience – it's a critical asset in scaling smartly and sustainably.

### Maintain Work-Life Balance

Equally important is maintaining your work-life balance as you scale. Set realistic growth goals that align with your personal energy and capacity, not just your financial ambition. Give yourself permission to schedule breaks and time off to recharge – burnout can quietly erode even the most successful investment plans. And don't hesitate to delegate or outsource the tasks that drain your time or fall outside your zone of expertise. Protecting your well-being isn't just a personal win – it's a leadership decision that ensures your business grows with strength and resilience.

### Review and Adjust Strategies

Part of scaling wisely includes stepping back to review and refine your strategy. Conducting regular portfolio reviews allows you to evaluate performance, identify what's working, and spot areas needing improvement. As you gain more experience, be willing to adjust your acquisition criteria and operational processes based on lessons learned. What made sense at twenty units may no longer apply at 200. Staying flexible, curious, and open to evolving your business model helps you avoid building a business that no longer fits the life you want.

## Conclusion

As you grow, remember that scale magnifies everything – your systems, your strengths, and your shortcomings. That's why it's critical to be intentional about how you grow. Build a foundation rooted in clarity, supported by capable partners, and powered by efficient tools. When done right, scaling your portfolio doesn't just increase your unit count – it expands your freedom, your impact, and your legacy. Let growth serve your life – not consume it.

## Reflection Questions

1. What systems and processes do you currently have in place for managing your properties?
2. Where are the gaps that could slow your growth?
3. Are you leveraging partnerships or joint ventures to expand your capital and expertise?
4. What steps can you take to build or strengthen these relationships?
5. Have you explored refinancing options to recycle equity from existing properties?
6. How comfortable are you with the timing and risks involved?
7. What roles do you currently fulfill in your business that could be delegated or outsourced?
8. How can building a team free you up to focus on growth and strategy?
9. How do you stay informed about best practices and market changes related to scaling multifamily investments?
10. What metrics or KPIs do you track across your portfolio to monitor performance and inform decisions?
11. What is your biggest challenge or fear about scaling your portfolio?
12. How can you begin to address it today?
13. Do you have a clear vision of your portfolio size and goals over the next three to five years?
14. What is one actionable step you can take this month toward that vision?

# CHAPTER 16:
# LEGAL CONSIDERATIONS AND COMPLIANCE – PROTECTING YOUR INVESTMENT BY NAVIGATING LAWS AND REGULATIONS

*"Compliance does not foster innovation, trust does."*
— Stephen R. Covey

Investing in multifamily real estate comes with significant responsibilities – not just to your tenants and partners but also to the laws and regulations that govern property ownership and management. Failure to comply with legal requirements can lead to costly lawsuits, fines, delays, and damage to your reputation. This chapter equips you with an essential understanding of key legal areas: landlord-tenant laws, fair housing regulations, building and safety codes, and best practices for maintaining compliance.

## Understanding Landlord-Tenant Laws

Let me share a quick story that made one of my clients rethink how crucial legal compliance is, especially when it comes to landlord-tenant laws. Early in his investing journey, he used a boilerplate lease agreement he had downloaded online – thinking all leases were pretty much the same. He didn't realize it lacked key clauses required by local regulations and didn't offer adequate protection for late payments or property damage. One tenant dispute later, he found himself in small claims court defending a situation he could have avoided entirely with a legally sound lease. After that wake-up call, he worked closely with a real estate attorney to revise every clause, ensuring compliance and clarity. That experience taught him the real value of solid legal infrastructure – not as a last resort, but as a proactive shield for everything he was building.

Landlord-tenant laws vary not only by state but often by municipality, and overlooking even a minor local regulation can result in costly disputes or delayed evictions – turning what looked like a great deal into a legal headache. I once knew an investor who purchased a promising duplex in a new city, only to discover too late that local rent control laws severely limited his ability to raise rents or remove nonpaying tenants. What started as a cash-flowing asset quickly became a financial drain.

Lease Agreements: Your lease is the foundation of your landlord-tenant relationship. It must comply with local laws, clearly outline rent amounts, due dates, security deposit terms, maintenance responsibilities, and eviction procedures.

Security Deposits: Laws regulate the maximum deposit amount, handling, and deadlines for returning deposits. Mismanaging deposits can lead to legal disputes.

Rent Control and Rent Stabilization: In some markets, rent increases and tenant evictions are tightly regulated. Understanding these rules helps avoid illegal rent hikes or unlawful eviction attempts.

Evictions: Proper eviction procedures are crucial. This involves giving tenants required notices, following court processes, and not engaging in "self-help" evictions (such as locking tenants out).

Maintenance and Habitability: Landlords must maintain rental units in safe, livable conditions. Failure to address repairs can result in tenant complaints or legal action.

Best Practice: Work with an experienced property attorney to draft and review lease forms and eviction processes that comply with your jurisdiction's requirements.

Stay current with changes in tenant law and local ordinances.

## Complying with Fair Housing Regulations

The Fair Housing Act, enacted in 1968 and later amended, is a federal law that prohibits discrimination in the sale, rental, and financing of housing based on race, color, national origin, religion, sex, familial status, or disability.

Its significance lies in its role as the foundation of equal housing opportunity in the United States. For multifamily investors, this law not only shapes marketing, screening, and tenant selection processes – it also carries serious legal and financial consequences if violated. A simple misstep, even if unintentional, can lead to complaints, investigations, fines, and reputational damage. Compliance isn't just about following the law – it's about building inclusive communities and protecting your business.

I recall a situation when I was screening applicants for one of my clients' properties and casually asked a prospective tenant if they had children – simply making conversation. I had no idea that this could be construed as a violation of the Fair Housing Act, which prohibits discrimination based on familial status among other protected characteristics like race, religion, sex, and disability. Luckily, I was gently corrected by a more experienced colleague before any damage was done, but it was a sobering moment. Since then, I've trained every leasing agent I work with to follow strict, consistent protocols during tenant interactions and always steer clear of language or questions that could be misinterpreted. That one moment taught me that compliance isn't just about avoiding fines – it's about building a reputation for fairness, professionalism, and trust in the communities we serve.

The Fair Housing Act and related state laws prohibit discrimination in housing based on protected characteristics such as race, color, religion, sex, national origin, disability, and familial status.

Advertising: Your marketing must be inclusive and not discourage any protected group.

Tenant Screening: Screening criteria must be applied uniformly to all applicants. Avoid questions or requirements that could be seen as discriminatory.

Reasonable Accommodations: For tenants with disabilities, landlords may be required to make reasonable modifications or accommodations (such as allowing **service animals).**

Avoiding Discriminatory Practices: Practices such as steering tenants to certain units or neighborhoods or charging different rent based on protected classes are illegal.

Consequences: Violations of fair housing laws can lead to lawsuits, hefty fines, and damage to your reputation.

Best Practice: Train your staff in fair housing rules and document all tenant interactions consistently. When in doubt, consult legal counsel to ensure compliance.

## Adhering to Building and Safety Codes

Adhering to local building and safety codes is equally important in protecting both your investment and the people who live in your properties. I once acquired a twenty-four-unit building that appeared to be in great shape – but soon after closing, I learned the previous owner had performed several unpermitted renovations, including replacing electrical systems without licensed contractors. What seemed like a minor oversight turned into a costly ordeal when the city required all the work to be redone and brought up to code. That experience taught me to always verify permits and compliance before closing. Whether it's ensuring proper fire exits, maintaining up-to-date smoke detectors, or complying with ADA accessibility requirements, staying ahead of these regulations prevents headaches, avoids fines, and, most importantly, keeps your tenants safe and your reputation intact.

Best Practice: Hire licensed contractors and obtain all necessary permits for renovations. Conduct regular inspections to ensure ongoing compliance and tenant safety.

## Environmental Compliance

Environmental compliance is another critical responsibility multifamily investors can't afford to overlook. I once considered buying a charming sixteen-unit property built in the early 1970s, unaware that environmental hazards could become a major liability. During due diligence, we discovered potential lead-based paint in several units, which required disclosure under EPA regulations. We also found mold in the basement – a serious health risk and a red flag for lenders. Fortunately, we acted early: hired an environmental inspector, remediated the issue, and implemented a lead disclosure protocol. This experience highlighted how essential it is to evaluate environmental risks up front. Whether it's addressing lead paint, asbestos, mold, or managing waste and hazardous materials properly, staying compliant protects your tenants, your investment, and your legal standing.

## Managing Legal Risks Proactively

Managing legal risks proactively is a non-negotiable aspect of scaling your multifamily portfolio. First, make sure you carry comprehensive landlord insurance that includes both liability and property coverage – it's your first line of defense. Equally important is documentation: maintain thorough, organized records of leases, tenant communications, maintenance requests, and payment histories. This paper trail is your safety net if disputes arise. Establishing a relationship with a seasoned real estate attorney is another critical move. Having someone you trust to draft leases, review contracts, and provide legal guidance can save you from costly missteps. Lastly, don't underestimate the value of ongoing staff training. Your property managers and leasing agents are on the front lines – ensure they understand fair housing laws, compliance protocols, and how to interact professionally and lawfully with tenants. Together, these steps form a proactive strategy that protects your business, enhances your credibility, and gives you peace of mind.

In my own experience, staying proactive with compliance hasn't just protected my investments; it's protected my peace of mind. By understanding landlord-tenant laws, fair housing regulations, building codes, and environmental requirements, you protect your investment from costly legal pitfalls and foster a professional, tenant-friendly operation. Staying informed, working with experts, and prioritizing transparent, fair practices are keys to navigating this complex but essential landscape.

## Legal Considerations and Compliance Checklist

### Landlord-Tenant Laws

Landlord-tenant laws form the backbone of your legal relationship with renters and must be followed diligently. One mistake I made early on was assuming a one-size-fits-all lease would cover everything – only to learn the hard way that local laws around security deposits, maintenance obligations, and eviction procedures vary widely. Now, every lease I use is reviewed by legal counsel and tailored to the property's jurisdiction. Make sure your agreements clearly outline all terms related to rent, deposits, repairs, and termination. If you operate in areas with rent control or stabilization laws, understand those limits thoroughly. Always follow formal eviction processes – avoiding shortcuts like self-help evictions, which can backfire legally. And above all, ensure that your units meet habitability standards with timely repairs and safe living conditions. Complying with landlord-tenant laws isn't just a legal requirement – it's a commitment to professionalism, fairness, and long-term success.

### Fair Housing Compliance

Fair Housing compliance is critical to operating a lawful and ethical multifamily investment business. All advertising and marketing must be inclusive and avoid language or imagery that could imply a preference or discourage protected groups. Every applicant must be evaluated using the same screening criteria – no exceptions. Provide reasonable accommodations when tenants have disabilities, such as allowing service animals or installing accessibility features. Just as important is ensuring your entire team – from leasing agents to maintenance staff – is regularly trained on Fair Housing laws and anti-discrimination policies. Keep meticulous records of all tenant communications and screening processes, as documentation can be your strongest defense if a claim arises. Ultimately, a commitment to Fair Housing isn't just about compliance – it's about cultivating a culture of fairness and respect in every property you manage.

### *Building and Safety Codes*

Building and safety code compliance is essential for protecting both your investment and your tenants. Before beginning any construction or renovations, always obtain the required permits and ensure all work meets current building code standards. Overlooking this step can result in fines or mandatory rework that can delay your project and eat into profits. Fire safety measures must also be strictly adhered to – this includes installing and regularly maintaining smoke detectors, providing accessible fire extinguishers, and ensuring all exits are unobstructed and clearly marked. Additionally, maintaining health and safety standards such as sanitation, pest control, water quality, and ventilation not only keeps tenants safe but prevents code violations that can affect property value and occupancy. Compliance with ADA and local accessibility requirements is also vital, especially in properties with public access or multiple tenants. Regular inspections and proactive maintenance help confirm ongoing compliance and minimize risks. When you prioritize building and safety standards, you're not just checking regulatory boxes – you're creating a safe, trustworthy environment that supports long-term investment success.

## *Environmental Compliance*

Environmental compliance is a critical responsibility for multifamily investors, particularly when acquiring older properties. Regulations such as those related to lead-based paint, asbestos, and mold are not just bureaucratic red tape – they exist to protect tenant health and investor liability. For properties built before 1978, federal law requires landlords to disclose any known lead-based paint hazards and provide tenants with an EPA-approved information pamphlet. Similarly, properties must be evaluated for potential asbestos or mold risks – both of which can pose serious health concerns and lead to costly legal action if ignored. I once considered purchasing a 1970s-era building that appeared solid on the surface, only to discover during due diligence that it had untreated mold in several units. That insight saved me from inheriting a future lawsuit and major cleanup costs. Moreover, proper waste disposal and the handling of hazardous materials – like cleaning agents or renovation debris – must follow local environmental guidelines. Proactive inspections and compliance measures not only shield your investment from fines and lawsuits, but also uphold your reputation as a responsible, ethical housing provider.

## *Risk Management*

Proactive risk management is essential as your portfolio grows in size and complexity. Start by maintaining robust landlord insurance that includes both property and liability coverage – this serves as a financial safety net in the event of accidents, natural disasters, or tenant-related issues. Just as important is your documentation system: keep meticulous records of leases, tenant communications, maintenance requests, and payments. In disputes, clear documentation often determines outcomes. Don't try to navigate compliance alone – work with a qualified real estate attorney to draft lease agreements, handle disputes, and ensure regulatory compliance. And remember, your team is only as strong as its understanding of the law. Provide ongoing legal training for property managers and leasing agents so they're equipped to handle tenant relations correctly. Effective risk management isn't just about avoiding problems – it's about protecting your assets, preserving your reputation, and operating with peace of mind.

## Legal Compliance Action Plan for Multifamily Investors

### Enhance Your Legal Knowledge

Enhancing your legal knowledge is a proactive step that protects your investments as your portfolio grows. Real estate law is dynamic – what you understood a year ago may no longer apply today. To stay ahead, schedule regular updates on landlord-tenant laws, fair housing regulations, and local ordinances relevant to the markets where you operate. Consider subscribing to legal newsletters, participating in webinars, or joining local real estate investor associations that offer timely legal alerts and insights. Staying informed isn't about becoming your own lawyer – it's about being a savvy investor who anticipates changes, avoids legal pitfalls, and leads with confidence.

### Review and Update Lease Agreements

Reviewing and updating your lease agreements annually is a smart and necessary part of scaling your portfolio. As laws evolve and your operations expand across different jurisdictions, outdated lease language can expose you to unnecessary legal risk. Working with a qualified real estate attorney ensures that your lease templates remain compliant with the latest landlord-tenant laws and that critical terms – like rent collection, security deposits, maintenance responsibilities, and eviction procedures – are clearly written and enforceable.

A well-crafted lease not only protects your rights as a landlord but also creates a foundation of clarity and professionalism that benefits both you and your tenants.

### *Standardize Security Deposit and Eviction Procedures*

To maintain consistency and legal compliance across your growing portfolio, it's essential to standardize how you handle security deposits and eviction processes. Develop clear, documented procedures that align with state and local laws – this includes how much you collect, how funds are held, timelines for returning deposits, and what deductions are permitted. Likewise, train your team on executing evictions properly, ensuring you follow legal steps such as notices, filings, and court proceedings. Avoid informal or "self-help" methods, which can expose you to lawsuits and damage your reputation. When everyone on your team understands and follows the same standardized process, you reduce liability, streamline operations, and protect both your business and your tenants' rights. Standardization frees you from guesswork and creates consistency as your team grows.

### *Ensure Fair Housing Compliance*

Ensuring fair housing compliance is not only a legal requirement – it's a cornerstone of ethical and sustainable property management. Every investor must implement clear policies for inclusive advertising and consistent, non-discriminatory tenant screening processes. Annual training for leasing and management staff is essential to reinforce awareness of Fair Housing laws and prevent unintentional violations. Just as critical is maintaining comprehensive documentation of tenant interactions, applications, and decisions. This transparency protects your business while demonstrating your commitment to equity. When fair housing becomes part of your company culture, you build not just a compliant business – but a respected and trustworthy one.

### *Maintain Property Safety and Code Compliance*

Maintaining property safety and compliance with local building codes isn't just about avoiding fines – it's about protecting your tenants, your investment, and your peace of mind. Begin by establishing a regular schedule for property inspections and preventative maintenance to catch small issues before they become expensive repairs. Always verify that any construction, renovations, or major repairs have the proper permits in place, as unpermitted work can lead to legal liabilities and forced rework. Periodically review fire safety systems – such as smoke detectors, extinguishers, and exit signage – and ensure that accessibility features meet ADA and local standards. Staying proactive in these areas not only builds tenant trust but also ensures the longevity and legal security of your portfolio.

### *Manage Environmental Risks*

Managing environmental risks is essential for maintaining both the safety of your properties and your legal standing as an investor. Start by conducting thorough environmental assessments during due diligence, especially for older properties that may contain hazards like lead-based paint or asbestos. If any environmental risks are identified, ensure they are disclosed to tenants as required by law and take swift action to remediate them. Mold, for example, can pose significant health issues and lead to costly lawsuits if ignored. Properly managing hazardous materials and waste disposal is also critical – many municipalities have strict regulations in place, and noncompliance can result in hefty fines or legal action. Proactively addressing these concerns not only protects your tenants and investment but also reinforces your reputation as a responsible and ethical operator.

### *Strengthen Risk Management*

To strengthen your risk management practices, make it a habit to review your insurance policies annually, ensuring they offer adequate coverage for both property damage and liability claims. A growing portfolio increases your exposure, and having the right protection in place is essential. Beyond insurance, meticulous recordkeeping becomes your safeguard – maintain organized, detailed logs of leases, rent payments, maintenance work, and all tenant interactions. These documents can serve as vital evidence in the event of a dispute or legal action. By proactively managing risk through preparation and documentation, you create a resilient foundation that supports sustainable, confident growth.

### *Establish Legal Partnerships*

Establishing legal partnerships is essential as your portfolio grows and legal complexity increases. Proactively identify and build relationships with experienced real estate attorneys who understand multifamily investing, local regulations, and transactional law. Set up regular consultations to review your compliance practices, address potential risks, and handle disputes promptly. Having a trusted legal advisor on your team not only strengthens your foundation but also gives you the confidence to navigate acquisitions, tenant issues, and regulatory changes with clarity and speed. When legal counsel is integrated into your strategic planning, it becomes not just an emergency contact but a long-term strategic partner you can rely on.

Navigating the legal landscape of multifamily investing is not just about avoiding lawsuits – it's about building a solid foundation for sustainable, scalable success. From lease agreements to risk management, as your portfolio grows, your legal responsibilities multiply. But with the right knowledge, systems, and professional guidance in place, compliance becomes a strategic advantage – not a burden. Treat the law not as a barrier but as a boundary that keeps your business strong, ethical, and future-ready.

## Conclusion

Legal compliance isn't just a box to check – it's a critical layer of protection for your investment, reputation, and long-term success. From fair housing laws and local ordinances to lease agreements and entity structures, understanding and following the rules ensures you avoid costly disputes, fines, or lawsuits. The most successful multifami ly investors stay informed, seek expert legal counsel, and build systems that keep their operations clean and compliant. When you take legal responsibilities seriously, you not only protect what you've built – you create a strong foundation for sustainable growth and peace of mind.

## Reflection Questions

1. How familiar are you with the landlord-tenant laws in the jurisdictions where you own properties?
2. What steps can you take to deepen your knowledge and stay current?
3. Do your lease agreements clearly outline all essential terms and comply with local legal requirements?
4. When was the last time you had them reviewed by a qualified attorney?
5. Are you consistently managing security deposits and eviction procedures according to applicable laws?
6. How do you ensure your marketing and tenant screening processes comply with Fair Housing laws?
7. What training or resources do you provide to your staff to maintain fair housing and non-discrimination compliance?
8. Are you regularly conducting inspections and maintaining properties to meet building and safety codes?
9. Do you have a process to obtain all necessary permits for construction and renovations?
10. Are you aware of any environmental hazards (lead paint, asbestos, mold) on your properties, and how are you managing them?
11. Do you maintain adequate insurance coverage to protect against legal and liability risks?
12. What relationships have you established with legal professionals to help you navigate compliance and disputes?

# CHAPTER 17:
# INVESTING ACROSS MARKETS

*"Don't wait to buy real estate. Buy real estate and wait."*
— Will Rogers

While many investors start close to home, the most successful ones know that opportunity often lies beyond their backyard. Markets differ dramatically in terms of affordability, job growth, rental demand, and landlord laws. For instance, Austin, Texas has seen explosive job growth in the tech sector, creating strong rental demand and rising rents – but affordability is shrinking as prices climb. In contrast, Cleveland, Ohio offers lower property prices and higher cash-on-cash returns, but slower population growth and more modest rent appreciation.

Then there's New York City, where strict rent regulations and tenant-friendly laws can tie a landlord's hands, even in high-demand neighborhoods. Compare that to Phoenix, Arizona, which has a more landlord-friendly legal environment and a growing population, making it attractive for long-term rental strategies.

The ability to evaluate and invest in the right markets – regardless of geography – is a skill that opens the door to greater returns, portfolio diversification, and long-term stability. Mastering this gives you the freedom to go where the opportunity is, not just where you live.

In this chapter, you'll learn how to assess new markets with confidence, understand the key metrics that matter, and build a strategy that balances local familiarity with national potential. Whether you're exploring your first out-of-state deal or planning to expand into multiple regions, this chapter will show you how to invest intelligently – anywhere opportunity calls.

One of the most common pieces of real estate advice is: "Invest where you live." And while there's wisdom in starting close to home – familiarity, easier management, local connections – your zip code shouldn't limit your wealth-building potential.

Some of the best deals may exist in cities you've never been to – places with better cash flow, faster growth, or more landlord-friendly laws. The key is knowing how to analyze a market objectively, identify promising locations, and build a local team to bridge the distance.

In this chapter, we'll explore how to evaluate real estate markets, what trends to follow, and how to confidently invest outside your home city – even across state lines or internationally.

## Local versus Out-of-State Investing

Investing locally offers the advantage of market familiarity, property access, and personal connections, but may come with challenges like high entry costs or limited opportunities depending on your area's growth and pricing dynamics.

Investing out-of-state can provide access to lower prices, stronger cap rates, and high-growth markets, but it demands deeper research, remote oversight, and a reliable local team to execute successfully. The decision isn't either/or – it's about strategy and scale. You may start local, then expand to stronger-performing markets as your confidence grows.

## How to Analyze a Real Estate Market

Before investing in any city, start by asking these essential questions to evaluate its true potential:

Analyzing a real estate market starts by assessing population growth trends using sources like U.S. Census data, local economic reports, and migration studies to determine whether an area is attracting new residents or experiencing decline. Is the population increasing? Are new people moving in, or are residents leaving?

I remember evaluating a mid-sized city in the Midwest that had once thrived on manufacturing. On paper, the home prices looked like a bargain. But a deeper dive into the data revealed a decade-long population decline, with more people moving out than in. Local job losses and stagnant wages were quietly draining demand. A friend of mine invested there without checking the migration trends – and within a year, he was struggling with high vacancy rates and no rental appreciation. A property can look like a great deal, but if people are leaving the area, the cash flow won't last.

Job growth and industry diversity are critical indicators of market stability, so look for BLS data, news of business expansions, and the presence of anchors like universities or hospitals to ensure the area isn't overly reliant on a single employer. Are new jobs being created? Are there multiple industries or just one major employer?

Rent and occupancy trends reveal the strength of a rental market, so track metrics like rent growth and vacancy rates using sources such as the Zillow Rent Index, Yardi Matrix, and local broker reports to gauge demand and income potential.

Affordability and cash flow are key to sustainable investing, so analyze price-to-rent ratios, GRM, and cap rates to ensure property values align with rental income and offer strong cash flow potential. Can the average person afford to rent or buy in the area? Are purchase prices in line with rental income?

Landlord-tenant laws vary widely by market, so it's essential to understand local eviction processes, rent control policies, and regulatory climate – and to consult a local attorney or property manager before investing. Are laws landlord-friendly or tenant-friendly? What are eviction timelines and rent control policies? Always consult a local attorney or property manager before investing in a new market.

Infrastructure and development projects – such as new roads, schools, transit, or revitalization efforts – are strong indicators of future appreciation, making them essential factors to evaluate when selecting a market. Is the city investing in roads, schools, public transportation, or revitalization? These improvements often drive appreciation.

When I began my real estate career in Manhattan, the market was highly competitive, international, and driven by appreciation. My clients made seven-figure investments in premier locations, and while the cash flow was modest, the long-term equity gains were significant.

When I expanded into Florida – especially Palm Beach County – I discovered a different kind of opportunity: affordable entry prices, higher cash flow, and landlord-friendly laws. I could buy more doors for less money and generate consistent monthly income. Both markets had value – but for different reasons.

Understanding the unique strengths and risks of each market allowed me to build a more balanced and resilient portfolio.

If you're investing out of state or out of region, you'll need to set yourself up for success. If you're new to a market, consider partnering with someone who already operates there.

Hot market ≠ good market – because high demand and rising prices may signal you're buying at the peak, it's often wiser to target emerging markets with strong fundamentals, such as new infrastructure, institutional growth, or corporate relocations that indicate long-term potential. Not every "hot" market is a smart place to invest. If prices are already inflated or rent growth is slowing, you may be buying at the top. Look for emerging markets with strong fundamentals that are still early in their growth curve.

## The Power of Geographic Diversification

Investing across markets reduces your risk. A recession in one region might not impact another. Different areas also move through real estate cycles at different times. By spreading your investments, you create stability, opportunity, and resilience.

The ability to invest across markets gives you the freedom to follow opportunities, not just convenience. When you understand how to evaluate population trends, job growth, rent dynamics, and local regulations, you can make informed decisions that reduce risk and enhance returns – no matter the location. With the right team and data at your side, geography becomes a tool, not a limitation.

## Conclusion

Investing across markets opens the door to greater opportunities, diversification, and higher returns – but it also requires deeper research, stronger systems, and trusted local partnerships. By understanding population trends, job growth, rent dynamics, affordability, and local laws, you can identify markets that align with your strategy and risk profile. Remember, a "hot" market isn't always the right market, and smart investors look beyond the headlines to find strong, sustainable growth. Whether local or out-of-state, success comes from combining data-driven decisions with disciplined execution and the right team on the ground.

## Investing Across Markets Checklist

### Market Research and Analysis

- Identify potential target markets based on economic growth, population trends, and rental demand.
- Analyze local real estate supply and demand dynamics, including vacancy rates and new construction.
- Evaluate local regulations, taxes, and landlord-

tenant laws.

- Research neighborhood-level data for safety, schools, amenities, and development plans.

## *Financial Evaluation*

- Compare cap rates, average rents, and operating expenses across markets.
- Factor in transaction costs, property management fees, and potential travel expenses.
- Assess financing options available in each market.
- Calculate expected cash flow, ROI, and risk-adjusted returns.

## *Building Local Relationships*

- Establish connections with local brokers, property managers, and contractors.
- Engage with local real estate investor groups or associations.
- Leverage technology for remote property management and communication.

## *Due Diligence*

- Conduct thorough property inspections or hire trusted local professionals.
- Review seller financials, tenant leases, and historical operating data carefully.
- Understand local market timing and seasonality factors.

## *Operational Planning*

- Develop a property management plan tailored to the local market.
- Set up reliable communication and reporting systems.
- Plan for contingency and emergency responses remotely.

### *Risk Management*

- Diversify investments across multiple markets to reduce localized risk.
- Stay updated on local political and economic developments.
- Prepare for currency or tax implications if investing internationally.

## Reflection Questions

1. Are you currently investing in your local market?
2. If so, what are the pros and cons you've experienced?
3. Does your local market align with your investment goals (e.g., cash flow, appreciation, landlord laws)?
4. If not, what are the limitations you're facing?
5. Have you considered investing in another city or state?
6. What's held you back from doing so up to now?
7. What characteristics define your ideal investment market?
8. (e.g., population growth, job growth, affordability, cash flow, business-friendly environment)
9. Which three markets would you like to research further?
10. Start by listing cities or regions that align with your investment identity and strategy.
11. Do you have any contacts or resources in those markets?
12. (Brokers, agents, property managers, investors, attorneys, etc.)
13. How confident are you in analyzing a new market based on data?
14. What resources do you need to feel more confident? (e.g., tools, mentorship, market reports)
15. How will you begin building a local team in a new market?

16. Outline the first two to three roles you would fill and where you might find those professionals.
17. Would you consider visiting your target market in person before investing there? Why or why not?
18. What is one action step you can take this week to explore a new market?
19. (e.g., research population trends, join a local real estate group, schedule a market visit)

# CHAPTER 18:
# CREATING A CULTURE OF EXCELLENCE IN PROPERTY MANAGEMENT

*"Excellence in property management is built on a foundation of trust, respect, and a relentless commitment to creating a thriving community."*

— Anonymous

In multifamily investing, your property management team is the frontline of your business. They interact with tenants daily, oversee maintenance, and represent your brand in the community. Creating a culture of excellence within your management team isn't just about enforcing rules – it's about fostering a tenant-focused environment that drives satisfaction, encourages long-term retention, and protects your asset's value.

This chapter explores how to build and sustain a management culture that elevates tenant experience and operational performance, ultimately strengthening your investment's success.

## Define Clear Values and Expectations

Start by setting the tone. A thriving property management culture doesn't happen by accident – it starts with clearly defined values that reflect your company's mission and are reinforced at every level of the organization. Core principles like putting tenants first, acting with integrity, taking accountability, and pursuing continuous improvement lay the groundwork for both day-to-day decisions and long-term performance. These values shape how your team communicates, solves problems, and serves residents. To ensure consistency, document your standards and embed them into the hiring process, training programs, and performance evaluations. When everyone operates from the same playbook, culture stops being a buzzword – and becomes your competitive edge

## Hire for Attitude and Fit, Not Just Skills

A few years ago, we were hiring a property management assistant at one of our multifamily communities. We had several applicants with years of experience in real estate, leasing systems, and tenant communications. But there was one resume that stood out – not because it was packed with qualifications, but because of a short cover letter attached.

It was from a woman named Tanya. She had no prior experience in real estate or property management. Her background was in hospitality – she had worked the front desk at a hotel chain for years. But her letter was heartfelt. She spoke about her passion for helping people feel "at home," how she loved solving problems quickly, and how she believed in treating every person with dignity, no matter their situation.

What stood out wasn't her résumé – it was her mindset. Tanya didn't just want a job; she saw this as a calling. And when she described how she once stayed late to comfort a guest who had just lost a loved one, I realized something important: experience can be gained, but heart like that is rare. That's what you build a team around.

We hired her – and within months, she became the property's most trusted point of contact. Residents lit up when they saw her. Complaints dropped. Retention improved. Tanya didn't just manage the property – she brought warmth and humanity to it. She reminded us that while skills are important, character is what truly elevates a community.

## Invest in Comprehensive Training

A well-trained team is the foundation of an efficient, high-performing property management company. Comprehensive onboarding sets the tone, introducing new hires to company values, tenant communication standards, and essential operational procedures. But training doesn't stop after the first week – ongoing development is key. Regular sessions on customer service, legal compliance, maintenance protocols, and technology tools keep staff sharp and up-to-date in a rapidly evolving industry. Scenario-based learning, including role-playing exercises, prepares team members for real-life challenges such as handling tenant disputes or emergency maintenance issues. When employees are equipped with the knowledge, tools, and confidence to act decisively and professionally, the entire organization runs smoother – and both tenant satisfaction and team morale rise

## Foster Open Communication and Feedback

Open communication is the lifeblood of a thriving property management culture. By creating clear channels for both staff and tenants to share their experiences, concerns, and ideas, companies build trust and drive continuous improvement. Regular team meetings provide a safe space to discuss challenges, celebrate successes, and brainstorm solutions collaboratively. For tenants, tools like surveys, suggestion boxes, or digital feedback forms offer a direct line to management. Most importantly, feedback isn't just collected – it's acted upon. When people see their input leading to real change, whether it's a new maintenance protocol or a community event they suggested, they feel heard, respected, and valued. This sense of inclusion strengthens both tenant satisfaction and team engagement.

## Recognize and Reward Excellence

Acknowledging hard work and celebrating achievements is essential to building a motivated, high-performing team. When team members feel seen and appreciated, their commitment deepens and their performance improves. Public recognition during staff meetings or through internal communications can go a long way in reinforcing positive behaviors and boosting morale.

At one property, we implemented a monthly "Resident Shout-Out" email that highlighted staff members who went above and beyond – like the maintenance tech who fixed a heating issue late on a snowy weekend, or the leasing agent who helped a nervous first-time renter feel at ease. Residents loved being part of the recognition process, and employees felt proud knowing their efforts were noticed not just by management, but by the people they served.

Incentive programs tied to key metrics – like tenant satisfaction, occupancy rates, or maintenance response times – create healthy accountability and inspire consistent excellence. Beyond financial rewards, offering professional development opportunities such as industry certifications, leadership training, or conference attendance shows employees that their growth matters. A culture of recognition not only retains top talent but also encourages everyone to bring their best to the job every day.

## Leverage Technology to Enhance Service

In today's fast-paced environment, technology is no longer optional – it's a strategic advantage. High-performing property management companies equip their teams with modern tools that streamline operations and elevate the tenant experience. Property management software enables real-time tracking of maintenance requests, ensuring transparency and accountability from submission to resolution. Online portals empower residents to pay rent, submit service requests, and stay updated on community news at their convenience. Meanwhile, mobile tools allow on-site staff to respond to issues immediately, access tenant information, and update work orders in the field. By embracing technology, companies increase efficiency, reduce response times, and deliver the kind of seamless service today's tenants expect.

## Build a Sense of Community

Creating a strong sense of community within a property doesn't just make it a nicer place to live – it fosters emotional safety and belonging, which are key drivers of resident satisfaction and long-term retention. When residents feel known, welcomed, and supported, they're more likely to take pride in their surroundings and stay longer. Hosting inclusive events, encouraging neighbor connections, and responding to concerns with empathy all help create an environment where people feel they matter. In a world where many feel isolated, your property can become more than just a place to live – it can become a place where people feel at home.

At one of our communities, we noticed a quiet older resident named Mr. Greene who rarely left his unit. After a team member invited him to a weekend coffee social, he not only attended – he stayed for hours, sharing stories and laughing with neighbors. From that day on, he became a regular presence at community events. Months later, he told our staff, "I haven't felt this connected since my wife passed away." That's the power of creating belonging – it turns buildings into communities and neighbors into friends.

Hosting regular events like seasonal gatherings, BBQs, or simple meet-and-greets helps tenants connect beyond their front doors and fosters a neighborly atmosphere. Encouraging communication through tenant groups or online platforms allows residents to share updates, offer support, and stay informed. When people know and care about their neighbors, they're more likely to take pride in their surroundings. By promoting shared responsibility for common areas and building relationships, property managers cultivate a culture where residents feel at home – and want to stay.

Creating a culture of excellence in property management is a continuous journey. When your team embodies values of respect, responsiveness, and accountability, tenants feel valued and cared for. This leads to higher retention, fewer costly issues, and a stronger, more profitable property. Investing in your people and fostering a tenant-first mindset is one of the best ways to protect and grow your multifamily investment.

## A Week in the Life of an Excellent Property Management Company. Leadership and Communication

An excellent property management company begins each week with intention. On Monday mornings, the leadership team kicks off with a brief huddle – reaffirming the company's core values and weekly service priorities. These meetings are more than just a checklist review; they're a chance to align the team around shared goals, celebrate small wins, and address any immediate challenges. Throughout the week, open lines of communication are maintained not only among staff but also with residents. Whether it's a quick Slack update from a maintenance lead or a thoughtful follow-up email to a tenant, transparency and responsiveness are at the heart of operations. By reinforcing a culture of open dialogue and shared purpose, leadership creates a workplace where everyone – staff and tenants alike – feels heard, respected, and empowered.

## Training and Development

At a top-tier property management company, training and development are ongoing priorities, not one-time events. New team members are welcomed with a structured onboarding program that immerses them in the company's culture, service standards, and performance expectations. This foundation sets the tone for excellence from day one. But the learning doesn't stop there – staff are regularly engaged in training sessions that sharpen their skills in customer service, conflict resolution, and property-specific knowledge. Leadership actively supports professional growth by encouraging participation in industry workshops, certifications, and mentorship opportunities. This investment in people pays off through a confident, capable team that not only knows how to handle daily operations but does so with professionalism and pride.

## Accountability and Recognition

Accountability is the backbone of any high-performing property management company. Clear, measurable performance standards are set for every role, and progress is reviewed consistently during team check-ins and one-on-one evaluations. Service request systems are in place to monitor response times and ensure no issue falls through the cracks – every ticket is tracked, and resolution times are analyzed for continuous improvement. But accountability doesn't stop at metrics; it's balanced with meaningful recognition. Team members who go above and beyond – whether resolving a tenant concern swiftly or contributing innovative ideas – are publicly acknowledged and rewarded.

At one of our properties, a maintenance tech named Luis noticed a trend in repeated service requests related to faulty HVAC units. Instead of simply fixing the same issue each time, he took the initiative to investigate further, eventually identifying a larger problem with outdated wiring in one of the buildings. He brought it to management's attention, suggested a cost-effective solution, and helped oversee the upgrade – all without being asked. At the next all-hands meeting, we surprised Luis with a "Problem Solver of the Month" award and a bonus. His eyes lit up, not because of the money, but because his effort had been noticed. Afterward, other team members began stepping up in new ways – proof that when accountability is matched with recognition, it inspires a ripple effect of excellence.

## Tenant Engagement and Community Building

A great property management company understands that tenants are more than just occupants – they're members of a community. Each week includes intentional efforts to build that sense of belonging, from organizing casual coffee mornings or seasonal events to celebrating holidays and local milestones. Feedback is continuously gathered through surveys, digital suggestion boxes, or informal conversations, giving residents a voice in how their living environment evolves. When concerns arise, they're addressed promptly and with genuine care, reinforcing trust and showing tenants that their comfort and satisfaction matter. By nurturing these relationships and fostering connection, the company transforms properties into welcoming, vibrant communities where people feel at home.

## Conflict Resolution and Professionalism

Even in the best-run communities, conflicts will arise – but how they're handled makes all the difference. An exceptional property management company equips its team with training in conflict resolution, active listening, and problem-solving, ensuring staff respond with calm, confidence, and empathy. Disputes between tenants or concerns about policies are addressed with fairness and consistency, guided by clearly established protocols that emphasize respect for all parties involved. This commitment to professionalism extends beyond individual incidents – it's woven into the culture, promoting an inclusive, supportive atmosphere where both tenants and team members feel valued and heard. By managing conflict thoughtfully, the company not only maintains harmony but also builds long-term trust across the community.

## Conclusion

Creating a culture of excellence in property management doesn't happen by chance – it's the result of intentional leadership, clear values, and consistent action. From hiring for attitude and investing in ongoing training to fostering tenant relationships and handling conflicts with professionalism, every detail matters. A thriving culture is one where team members feel empowered, tenants feel respected, and every interaction reflects a commitment to quality and care. When excellence becomes the norm, not the exception, your properties don't just perform better – they become places where people are proud to live and work. That's the true hallmark of a world-class property management company.

## Reflection Questions

1. How would you describe the current culture within your property management team?
2. What values and behaviors are most evident?
3. What practices do you have in place to foster trust and respect among your staff and tenants?
4. How do you communicate expectations and standards for service excellence to your team?
5. In what ways do you encourage accountability and continuous improvement within your management staff?
6. How effectively do you recognize and reward exceptional performance and tenant-focused behaviors?
7. What initiatives or programs do you offer to build a sense of community among tenants?
8. How do you handle conflicts or issues to maintain a positive and professional environment?
9. Are your training and onboarding processes aligned with the culture of excellence you want to create?
10. What feedback mechanisms are in place to listen to tenant and staff input for ongoing culture development?
11. What is one actionable step you can take today to strengthen your property management culture?

# CHAPTER 19:
# TECHNOLOGY, AI, AND
# THE FUTURE OF MULTIFAMILY

*"The future belongs to those who prepare for it today."*
— Malcolm X

## My Approach to Tech in Real Estate

Coming from a banking background, I've always valued data, precision, and analysis. As I built my real estate portfolio, I brought those same expectations to my investing approach.

Today, I use digital tools to help underwrite deals, streamline operations, and maintain high standards of communication with investors. For example, deal analysis platforms like RealPage or DealCheck allow me to run detailed financial models in minutes – evaluating cap rates, cash-on-cash returns, and value-add scenarios with far greater speed and accuracy than spreadsheets alone. This not only helps me act faster in competitive markets but also gives my investors confidence that every opportunity has been thoroughly vetted.

On the operations side, property management software like AppFolio or Buildium centralizes everything from rent collection and maintenance requests to accounting and reporting. This keeps the team aligned and ensures no detail falls through the cracks.

Leasing has also become more efficient with virtual

tour technology and online applications. Platforms like Rently or Matterport allow prospective tenants to tour units anytime, eliminating scheduling friction and widening your reach to more qualified applicants.

And when it comes to communication, investor portals such as Juniper Square or InvestNext make it easy to share updates, distribute reports, and maintain transparency – something today's investors value more than ever.

The future belongs to the informed, the agile, and the connected. Technology and AI are not just tools – they are catalysts for transformation in real estate investing. By staying curious and adopting innovations that enhance efficiency, accuracy, and transparency, you position yourself to seize opportunities others might miss. Remember, technology doesn't replace good judgment; it amplifies it. As you integrate these tools into your investing journey, you'll unlock new levels of growth, control, and impact. In the next chapter, we'll turn our attention to building a legacy – how your investments today can create lasting wealth and meaning for generations to come.

## Adopt Property Management Technology

As the multifamily industry evolves, embracing technology is no longer a competitive edge – it's a necessity. Modern property management software streamlines core functions like leasing, rent collection, and maintenance tracking into a single, integrated platform, reducing administrative burdens and improving operational visibility. AppFolio has been a game-changer when it comes to automating rent collection and reducing delinquencies. With features like autopay enrollment, automated late fee postings, and tenant reminders, I've seen on-time payments increase significantly across properties. Tenants appreciate the convenience of paying online, and my team spends less time chasing payments or handling manual bookkeeping. Plus, the real-time financial dashboards give me instant visibility into property performance – allowing for faster, data-driven decisions.

Digital communication tools allow tenants to submit service requests, receive updates, and interact with management quickly and conveniently. Automation plays a key role in reducing human error and freeing up staff time for higher-value tasks, such as tenant engagement and strategic planning. By adopting and continually evaluating the latest tools, property management companies position themselves to run more efficiently, serve tenants better, and scale operations with confidence.

## A Story of Transformation Through Technology

One of my clients managed a 120-unit multifamily property the old-fashioned way – paper leases, handwritten maintenance logs, rent checks dropped in a physical box. While the team was dedicated, inefficiencies piled up. Maintenance requests were often delayed because the paperwork got misplaced, and rent reconciliation took days at the end of every month. Residents grew frustrated, and staff were stretched thin.

That all changed when he made the decision to invest in a comprehensive property management software platform. Within weeks, everything from lease renewals to maintenance tracking was digitized. Tenants could now log service requests through an app and get real-time updates on the status. Rent payments became seamless through an online portal, and automated reminders drastically reduced late payments. His staff had access to dashboards that tracked performance metrics, upcoming tasks, and tenant communications in one place.

But the most unexpected benefit was the shift in tenant satisfaction. Residents appreciated the transparency and faster response times. Maintenance teams were better organized, and leasing staff could focus more on building relationships rather than chasing paperwork. One resident even said, "It feels like we moved into the Twenty-First century overnight."

The investment in technology not only made his operations more efficient – it transformed his culture. It gave his team confidence, empowered residents, and turned an overburdened process into a streamlined, modern experience. It was a turning point that continues to pay dividends.

## Leverage Data Analytics and AI

The future of multifamily property management is being shaped by data and artificial intelligence. By leveraging AI-powered tools, companies can analyze market trends in real time, optimize rent pricing based on demand and competition, and make smarter, data-driven investment decisions. Predictive analytics go a step further – helping anticipate maintenance issues before they become costly repairs, reducing downtime and improving tenant satisfaction. On the front end, AI-driven chatbots and virtual assistants provide instant responses to tenant inquiries, schedule tours, and even handle basic service requests around the clock. When used thoughtfully, data and AI don't just enhance operational efficiency – they deliver a better, faster, and more personalized experience for both tenants and property managers. However, AI is only as good as the data behind it!

## A Data-Driven Turnaround

Faced with high turnover, rising costs, and stagnant rent growth, a client managing a ninety-unit property shifted from gut instinct to smart systems powered by AI and data. By implementing rent optimization software, predictive maintenance tools, and a tenant-facing AI chatbot, he boosted rent revenue by 6 percent, cut equipment downtime by 40 percent, and reduced repair costs by a third. The result? Happier tenants, a more efficient team, and a property that practically ran itself. This transformation proved that data isn't just helpful – it's essential for staying competitive in today's multifamily market.

## Integrate Smart Building Technologies

By integrating smart technologies, property owners not

only enhance the tenant experience but also increase asset value and operational resilience. At one newer development we managed, we decided to fully integrate smart building technologies from the ground up. Each unit was equipped with smart thermostats that allowed residents to control temperatures remotely – leading to fewer complaints and lower utility usage during peak seasons. In common areas, we installed motion-sensor LED lighting and energy-efficient systems that automatically adjusted based on occupancy and natural light, cutting shared electricity costs by nearly 25 percent.

We also replaced traditional keys with a smart access control system that gave residents app-based entry to their units, amenities, and package rooms. This not only improved convenience but also tightened security – allowing us to monitor access logs and respond quickly to any unusual activity.

The biggest payoff came when IoT leak sensors detected a slow water drip behind a wall in a vacant unit. Left unnoticed, it could have caused thousands in mold remediation and repairs. But thanks to real-time alerts, we caught it early and fixed it within hours.

The result was a modern, secure, and energy-efficient property that attracted tech-savvy tenants and commanded premium rents – all while lowering operating expenses and future-proofing the asset.

## Enhance Marketing and Leasing with Technology

Technology has revolutionized the way multifamily properties are marketed and leased. Virtual tours and 3D modeling now allow prospective tenants to explore units from anywhere, reducing barriers and accelerating leasing decisions. AI-driven marketing platforms analyze data to target the right audiences with personalized ads, helping attract high-quality tenants more efficiently. Meanwhile, online application and screening tools streamline the leasing process – cutting down on paperwork, minimizing delays, and ensuring a smooth, professional experience from first click to signed lease. We saw this firsthand when we implemented a full digital leasing system at one of our properties with historically high vacancy rates. Within three months, virtual tours and automated marketing campaigns helped reduce average vacancy time from twenty-seven days to just twelve. The result wasn't just faster leasing – it was happier tenants and a stronger bottom line.

## Prioritize Cybersecurity and Data Privacy

In an increasingly digital property management environment, safeguarding tenant and business data is not optional – it's essential. Implementing strong cybersecurity measures, such as firewalls, encryption, and multi-factor authentication, protects sensitive information from breaches and cyber threats. Compliance with data privacy regulations like GDPR and CCPA is equally critical, especially when collecting and storing tenant applications, payment information, and communication records. But technology alone isn't enough – staff must also be trained regularly on data security best practices, including how to recognize phishing attempts and manage sensitive data responsibly. By making cybersecurity a core operational priority, property management companies build trust, reduce liability, and ensure long-term digital resilience.

## Plan for Continuous Technology Adoption

Technology in property management is evolving rapidly, and staying ahead requires a mindset of continuous learning and adaptation. Forward-thinking companies make it a priority to stay informed about emerging tools, PropTech innovations, and industry trends that can enhance operations and tenant experiences. This includes allocating part of the annual budget specifically for technology upgrades and ongoing staff training to ensure teams are equipped to use new tools effectively. Collaborating with tech providers, attending industry conferences, and joining professional groups fosters innovation and keeps your company at the forefront of change. By planning proactively, property managers can avoid falling behind and ensure their operations remain efficient, competitive, and future-ready.

Real estate is evolving – and those who embrace innovation will lead the way. From AI-powered deal analysis to property management platforms that automate everything from rent collection to maintenance requests, technology is transforming how we invest, scale, and succeed.

In this chapter, we'll explore the tools and trends that are reshaping the multifamily landscape. You'll discover how to leverage technology not just for convenience, but as a strategic advantage. Whether you're managing a small portfolio or scaling into larger properties, understanding the tech behind the transaction can help you move faster, operate smarter, and stay competitive in a fast-changing market.

Real estate has traditionally been viewed as a slow-moving, relationship-driven industry. But over the past decade – and especially in recent years – technology has become a disruptive force reshaping every aspect of investing, managing, and scaling real estate portfolios.

Whether you're sourcing deals, underwriting properties, managing tenants, or forecasting performance, the rise of AI, automation, and data-driven tools has created a competitive edge for investors who embrace innovation.

In this chapter, we'll explore how technology is transforming multifamily real estate – and how you can use these advancements to increase efficiency, improve decision-making, and future-proof your portfolio.

## AI and Data in Deal Analysis

Artificial Intelligence (AI) is changing how we analyze deals. What used to take days – pulling comps, calculating returns, estimating repair costs – can now be done in minutes using smart platforms.

### AI-driven tools can:

AI-driven tools are transforming how multifamily investors identify, analyze, and execute deals. These platforms can rapidly scan and underwrite hundreds of listings, pinpointing the best investment opportunities based on your criteria. They leverage real-time data to estimate rent comps and property values with greater accuracy than traditional methods. Beyond the basics, AI can detect red flags in financial statements, market trends, or neighborhood metrics that might otherwise be overlooked. Perhaps most powerfully, AI can forecast future cash flow and potential appreciation – helping you evaluate long-term upside and mitigate risk before making an offer. With AI as your partner, you gain speed, clarity, and a strategic edge in a highly competitive market.

### Popular platforms include:

PropStream is a powerful property data and lead generation platform widely used by real estate investors and professionals. It provides comprehensive nationwide data on properties, including ownership information, mortgage details, tax assessments, and liens. The platform's strength lies in its ability to help investors identify off-market deals, analyze property values, and segment targeted mailing lists for direct outreach. Features like customizable filters and integrated comps make PropStream especially useful for sourcing multifamily opportunities that meet your specific criteria.

Mashvisor simplifies the property search and analysis process by providing real estate data analytics with a focus on rental property performance. It offers metrics such as occupancy rates, cash flow projections, cap rates, and comparative market analysis, drawing data from traditional and Airbnb rental markets. For multifamily investors, Mashvisor delivers heat maps that visualize high-performing neighborhoods and units, helping you identify lucrative markets quickly. Its intuitive interface is designed to save time and increase confidence in investment decisions.

DealCheck is an easy-to-use real estate analysis software that enables investors to quickly evaluate rental properties, fix-and-flip deals, and multifamily investments. It calculates key investment metrics like cash flow, ROI, cap rate, and internal rate of return (IRR) using inputted or imported data. Its mobile-friendly app allows investors to analyze deals on the go. DealCheck also supports side-by-side property comparisons, helping you prioritize opportunities and make informed offers.

Roofstock is an online marketplace specializing in turnkey single-family and small multifamily rental properties. It allows investors to buy fully leased properties remotely, complete with verified inspection reports and tenant information. Roofstock's platform streamlines the acquisition process by providing due diligence tools, transparent pricing, and access to property management services. For investors seeking passive income with lower operational involvement, Roofstock offers a turnkey solution to quickly add rental assets to their portfolio.

REoptimizer is a commercial real estate management and optimization platform designed for investors and asset managers handling larger multifamily or commercial portfolios. It integrates lease management, budgeting, tenant communications, and maintenance workflows into one dashboard. REoptimizer's data analytics capabilities enable users to track property performance, forecast income, and identify operational efficiencies. Its scalable design makes it suitable for growing investors who want to manage multiple properties with precision and insight.

These tools allow investors to move faster and with greater confidence, reducing guesswork and emotion from decision-making.

If you're just getting started, try experimenting with two smart tools side-by-side — like a leak detection sensor and a smart thermostat — to see firsthand how small upgrades can make a big impact without overwhelming your team or your budget.

## Property Management Tech

Owning multiple units or investing remotely can get overwhelming without the right systems. That's where property technology steps in.

### *Smart property management software can help you:*

Smart property management software is a game-changer for landlords and operators looking to streamline operations and scale efficiently. These platforms automate routine but essential tasks like rent collection, late fee notifications, and tenant reminders – ensuring consistency and reducing human error. All tenant communications can be managed in one centralized dashboard, improving response times and keeping records organized. Maintenance requests are easily tracked from submission to completion, with integrated vendor coordination to ensure accountability. Additionally, real-time financial reporting provides instant insights into cash flow, expenses, and performance metrics, empowering you to make informed decisions quickly. With the right software, you can save time, reduce stress, and run your properties with greater precision and professionalism.

### *Common platforms include:*

AppFolio is comprehensive, cloud-based property management software designed for portfolios of all sizes. It offers features such as online rent collection, maintenance request tracking, tenant screening, and robust accounting tools. Its user-friendly interface and mobile app allow landlords and property managers to efficiently manage operations from anywhere. AppFolio's scalability and extensive reporting capabilities make it a favorite for managing multifamily properties and larger residential portfolios.

Buildium is a powerful property management platform tailored to streamline operations for residential and association properties. It supports online leasing, payment processing, tenant communication, and maintenance workflows. Buildium also provides financial reporting and compliance tools that help property managers stay organized and transparent. With a focus on customer support and integration capabilities, Buildium is well-suited for property managers seeking an all-in-one solution.

RentRedi is a mobile-first property management app ideal for small to mid-sized landlords. It simplifies rent collection with automated reminders and offers features like digital lease signing, maintenance tracking, and tenant screening. RentRedi's intuitive design and affordability make it a practical choice for self-managing landlords who want to automate routine tasks and improve tenant communication without a steep learning curve.

Hemlane is a hybrid property management platform designed specifically for remote landlords. It combines technology with local support by connecting landlords to property managers and maintenance professionals in the property's area. Hemlane offers online rent collection, tenant screening, maintenance coordination, and leasing assistance — all accessible through a centralized dashboard. Its blend of automation and on-the-ground service helps investors manage properties efficiently from anywhere.

In addition, smart home tech — like keyless entry, smart thermostats, and remote security monitoring — can increase tenant satisfaction and lower operating costs.

## Virtual Tours, Leasing, and Marketing

The leasing process has fully embraced the digital age, meeting the expectations of today's renters who prefer convenience, speed, and flexibility. Freeing up leasing staff time improved tenant interactions or created more space for relationship-building.

With 3D virtual tours, prospective tenants can walk through a unit from anywhere in the world — perfect for out-of-town relocations or busy professionals. AI-powered chatbots provide instant responses to inquiries, keeping prospects engaged while reducing the burden on leasing staff. Online leasing platforms now support e-signatures and automated screening, enabling renters to tour, apply, and sign a lease entirely online. This streamlined process not only reduces vacancy time but also expands your reach to a broader, tech-savvy tenant pool – particularly valuable for Class A and urban multifamily properties where speed and first impressions make all the difference.

## Investor Portals and Reporting

In today's multifamily landscape, transparency and trust are essential – especially when raising capital and managing multiple investor relationships. Investor portals simplify this process by providing a secure, centralized hub for communication and reporting. These platforms allow you to share detailed financial reports, upload deal documents, and issue distributions with just a few clicks. Investors can log in anytime to track their individual IRR, cash flow, and performance metrics, reducing the need for back-and-forth emails. By offering real-time access to data and consistent updates, investor portals not only meet compliance standards but also strengthen credibility and investor confidence – making it easier to raise capital for your next deal. Investor portals and reporting make it easier for investors to stay informed and feel connected to the performance of their capital.

### *Popular investor portals include:*

Juniper Square is a leading investor management platform designed for real estate syndicators and fund managers. It streamlines investor onboarding, automates distributions, and provides detailed reporting. The platform offers secure document storage, performance tracking, and communication tools, making it easier to maintain transparency and build trust with investors.

InvestNext is a user-friendly investor portal tailored to real estate sponsors managing private equity investments. It facilitates investor relations by offering secure access to investment documents, distribution tracking, and real-time updates on portfolio performance. Its intuitive interface helps sponsors keep investors informed and engaged throughout the lifecycle of the investment.

Groundbreaker is an all-in-one platform combining investor management, deal management, and crowdfunding capabilities. It supports capital raising, subscription document management, and investor communications in one place. Groundbreaker's comprehensive tools simplify complex syndications and enhance operational efficiency for real estate sponsors.

These tools increase transparency, professionalism, and trust – especially for syndicators and capital raisers. For investors raising capital, tools like these don't just simplify logistics – they strengthen your reputation.

## Construction and Renovation Tech

For value-add investors and property managers overseeing renovations, construction technology is transforming how projects are executed – bringing greater control, visibility, and efficiency. Modern platforms now offer real-time project timelines, allowing you to monitor progress across multiple sites and catch delays early. Integrated budget tracking tools flag overruns and change orders instantly, helping you stay on top of costs and avoid surprise expenses. Centralized communication features streamline collaboration with contractors, architects, and vendors, while file sharing ensures everyone has access to the latest plans and documents. By leveraging these tools, you can complete renovations faster, within budget, and with fewer headaches – ultimately accelerating the return on your investment.

## Apps for Managing Renovation Projects

Buildertrend, CoConstruct, and Trello are powerful tools that help investors and property managers efficiently oversee small to midsize renovation projects from anywhere. These platforms offer features such as project timelines, budgeting, task assignment, and real-time communication with contractors and vendors. By centralizing all renovation details, they reduce miscommunication, keep projects on schedule and within budget, and provide transparency throughout the process. Whether you're managing a single property rehab or multiple upgrades, these apps help you stay organized, save time, and make informed decisions remotely.

## The Role of Predictive Analytics

AI in multifamily property management is moving beyond automation – it's becoming predictive. With the help of machine learning, today's advanced tools can forecast maintenance issues before they arise, allowing for proactive repairs that save money and prevent tenant frustration. Predictive models can also assess tenant behavior to estimate the likelihood of lease renewals, enabling managers to take early action to retain high-value residents. Dynamic rent pricing algorithms adjust rates in real time based on current market conditions, while long-term forecasts analyze local development trends to project future property values. By leveraging these insights, property managers can protect net operating income (NOI), reduce risk, and make smarter decisions that enhance both performance and asset value.

## What This Means for You

You don't need to be a tech expert to benefit from the new wave of property management technology – but you do need to stay open to change. The multifamily investors and operators who will thrive in the years ahead are those who remain curious, proactive, and willing to experiment with emerging tools. Whether it's testing a new leasing platform, automating maintenance workflows, or using data to guide pricing decisions, the goal isn't perfection – it's progress. By embracing innovation with a mindset focused on efficiency, accuracy, and transparency, you position yourself to build smarter systems, increase profitability, and create a better experience for your team and your tenants alike.

Technology doesn't replace sound judgment – it enhances it. It helps you scale faster, manage smarter, and serve your investors and tenants better.

## Conclusion

The integration of technology and AI is no longer a distant vision – it's a present-day imperative for multifamily property management. From streamlining operations and improving tenant engagement to enhancing security and enabling data-driven decision-making, technology offers powerful tools to elevate every aspect of your business. But success doesn't come from simply adopting the latest gadgets; it comes from building a culture that embraces continuous innovation, strategic investment, and ongoing learning. By staying agile, investing in your team, and aligning technology with your values and goals, you position your company not just to keep up with change – but to lead it. The future of multifamily is smart, responsive, and deeply human – and those who embrace it today will thrive tomorrow.

## Reflection Questions

1. How would you describe your current comfort level with using technology in your real estate business?
2. (Beginner, moderate, advanced)
3. Which part of your real estate investing process could benefit most from automation or smarter tools?
4. (e.g., deal analysis, property management, leasing, investor reporting)
5. Have you used any AI or data-driven platforms to evaluate real estate deals?
6. If not, which ones would you like to explore?
7. Are you currently using any property management software?

8. If so, what are the pros and cons? If not, what's holding you back?

9. What tools are you using – or could you begin using – to improve communication and transparency with investors?

10. Have you explored smart home technologies for your properties (e.g., keyless entry, smart thermostats)?

11. How might these impact your tenant experience and operational efficiency?

12. Do you feel you have the right systems in place to scale your portfolio efficiently?

13. If not, what's one area where better tech could make a difference?

14. What is one piece of real estate technology you'll commit to researching or testing this month?

15. How will you stay informed about new innovations and trends in real estate tech going forward?

16. (Podcasts, newsletters, meetups, conferences?)

17. What's your mindset around innovation – do you resist change, cautiously explore, or actively embrace new tools?

18. How might shifting your mindset improve your investing results?

# CHAPTER 20:
# LEAVING A LEGACY
# THROUGH REAL ESTATE

*"Carve your name on hearts, not tombstones. A legacy is etched into the minds of others and the stories they share about you."*
— Shannon L. Alder

Real estate can build wealth. But more importantly, it can build a legacy.

Real estate investing is about more than financial gain — it's about creating something that lasts beyond your lifetime. Legacy is the combination of the wealth, values, and impact you leave behind for your family and community.

In this chapter, we'll explore how to align your investments with your deeper purpose, involve your family in the journey, and build systems that preserve and grow your wealth across generations. Whether you're focused on cash flow, appreciation, or social impact, understanding legacy gives your investing greater meaning and direction.

A legacy isn't just about what you leave behind, it's about how you live today. It's about using your success not only to benefit yourself, but to uplift your family, your community, and even generations you'll never meet.

For many investors, the journey begins with cash flow and grows into a calling. After the first few properties and a handful of passive income checks, the question changes from *"How much can I earn?"* to *"What am I building – and for whom?"*

In this chapter, we'll explore how to use real estate as a tool for lasting impact, how to involve your family in the process, and how to align your investments with your values and vision.

## What Is Legacy?

Legacy is more than wealth – it's the values, habits, and impact you leave behind through real estate, whether by passing on a cash-flowing portfolio, teaching financial literacy, supporting charitable causes, mentoring others, or creating lasting value in your community.

## The Three Pillars of Impactful Investing

Every multifamily investor begins with a clear goal: financial freedom. It's the first pillar – the foundation that creates stability, options, and the ability to step off the treadmill of trading time for money. But for those who stay the course, financial freedom becomes a stepping stone, not the finish line.

The second pillar is **generational wealth** – not just accumulating assets, but building systems, values, and strategies that endure. It's where your portfolio evolves into a legacy, empowering future generations with knowledge, income, and opportunity.

And finally, at the height of this journey comes **purpose-driven investing** – the third pillar. Once your personal needs are met and your family is secure, you unlock the ability to invest with intention: revitalizing communities, supporting causes you care about, and using real estate as a tool for meaningful change.

This progression – from freedom, to legacy, to impact – is the true power of multifamily investing. And when you understand how these pillars connect, every decision you make can move you closer to the life and legacy you envision.

### 1. Financial Freedom

Creating recurring income from rental properties means you – and eventually your family – aren't dependent on a job or a fixed income.

It gives you:

- Time freedom to focus on what matters most
- The ability to take care of loved ones
- Resources to invest in experiences, education, or causes you care about

### 2. Generational Wealth

Real estate can appreciate in value, offer tax advantages, and be passed on through careful estate planning.

Strategies to consider:

- Setting up LLCs or family trusts
- 1031 exchanges to preserve capital
- Equipping your kids or beneficiaries to lead, manage and oversee assets
- Working with estate attorneys and CPAs to minimize tax burdens

### 3. Purpose-Driven Investing

Some of the most fulfilling real estate projects come from serving a mission: providing quality housing, restoring neglected properties, or supporting local economies.

You can design your portfolio around:

- Impact investing (e.g., affordable housing, green buildings)
- Community revitalization
- Education and mentorship through your real estate journey

## Involving Your Family in the Process

Your legacy is stronger when your family understands it – and participates in it. Here's how to bring them in:

- Share your vision: Let your children or heirs know why you invest and what your goals are.
- Teach the business: Involve them in property

tours, budgeting, or tenant interactions.

- Start small together: Consider a JV or small investment with a child or relative to pass on skills.
- Celebrate milestones: Treat real estate success as a family achievement, not just a personal one.
- Even if they don't become full-time investors, they'll carry the mindset and tools forward.

## My Legacy Journey

After decades in corporate banking, I turned to real estate not only as a second career – but as a way to invest in my family's future. I've worked with clients who made seven-figure investments, and I've built a personal portfolio that reflects my values and long-term goals.

But what I'm most proud of isn't the number of deals. It's watching my family become more financially literate, more confident, and more engaged in building something meaningful. It's knowing that the work I'm doing today will continue to support the people I love – and perhaps others I'll never meet.

That's what legacy is to me: income with intention. Ownership with purpose. Success that outlives you. And it's worth every bit of effort.

## Practical Legacy Planning Tips

- Set up an estate plan that includes wills, trusts, and clear asset transfer instructions.
- Work with a CPA who understands wealth preservation and generational tax strategy.
- Keep organized records of your investments, contacts, passwords, and legal documents.
- Create a letter of instruction or even a short video message to communicate your vision and wishes personally such as a love letter or reflection.
- Consider writing a family wealth mission statement that defines your values and goals as stew-

ards of wealth.

## Conclusion

Leaving a legacy is about intentionality – making choices today that will benefit your loved ones and community tomorrow. It requires planning, education, and a commitment to values beyond dollars and cents. When your real estate investments reflect who you are and what you stand for, they become more than assets; they become a powerful force for good. As you move forward, remember that your legacy is shaped not just by what you build, but by how you live and lead. In the final chapter, we'll wrap up this journey with a clear road map to help you take confident, consistent steps toward your real estate goals.

## Leaving a Legacy Through Multifamily Real Estate Checklist

### *Define Your Legacy Goals*

- Clarify what legacy means to you (financial security, family wealth, community impact).
- Set specific, measurable goals for your real estate portfolio and philanthropic efforts.

### *Estate Planning*

- Work with estate planning professionals to create or update wills and trusts.
- Consider setting up family limited partnerships or LLCs for property ownership.
- Plan for smooth transfer of assets to heirs with minimal tax consequences.

### *Education and Involvement*

- Educate family members about real estate investing and financial management.
- Involve heirs in property management or investment decisions early.
- Create documentation and guides for managing the portfolio. Encourage your heirs or succes-

sors to not only understand your real estate holdings but also how to manage them. Create both physical and digital copies of key documents – such as property deeds, loan agreements, and operating procedures – and consider recording video walkthroughs to explain your intentions, systems, and lessons learned. This personal touch can provide clarity, reduce confusion, and ensure your legacy is preserved and honored long after you're gone.

## *Philanthropy and Community Impact*

- Identify charitable causes or community projects aligned with your values.
- Explore opportunities for real estate donations or impact investing.
- Establish foundations or scholarship funds if desired.

## *Portfolio Management for Longevity*

- Maintain diversified and well-managed properties to sustain income over generations.
- Regularly review and adjust investment strategies to adapt to changing markets.
- Implement professional management to ensure continuity.

## *Communication and Transparency*

- Maintain open communication with family and stakeholders about goals and plans.
- Document legacy plans clearly and update as needed.

## Reflection Questions

1. What does the word "legacy" mean to you personally?
2. How do you want to be remembered by your family, community, or future generations?

3. In what ways can real estate help you build and sustain that legacy?
4. Think beyond wealth – consider values, impact, and long-term vision.
5. Have you talked with your family about your real estate goals and why you're pursuing them?
6. If not, when and how could you start that conversation?
7. How involved are your children, spouse, or heirs in your investing activities?
8. What small role or responsibility could you invite them into?
9. What are three lessons or principles about money, ownership, or investing you want to pass on?
10. Have you taken steps to create an estate plan, will, or trust that protects and transfers your real estate assets?
11. If not, what's one step you can take this month to begin that process?
12. Do your current investments reflect your values and the kind of impact you want to make?
13. If not, how might you shift your portfolio to align more closely with your purpose?
14. What organizations, causes, or communities could benefit from your success as an investor?
15. (e.g., mentorship, housing initiatives, charitable giving)
16. How will you ensure your wealth does not just get passed down – but your wisdom, too?
17. What is one action you can take this week to move closer to building a legacy through real estate?
18. (e.g., write down your legacy goals, involve a family member, consult with an estate planner)

# CHAPTER 21:
# CLIENTS' STORIES, REAL LESSONS

*"Experience is the teacher of all things."*
— Julius Caesar

## Reflections: Lessons Through Stories and Case Studies

At Harvard Business School, they taught us that the best learning often comes from studying real-world cases – where strategy meets uncertainty, and character is revealed in decisions. That stuck with me.

In the pages ahead, I'll share stories from clients whose journeys in multifamily real estate offer powerful lessons – some inspiring, some cautionary, all real. These case studies aren't just about numbers; they're about mindset, resilience, and the choices that shape success.

As we wrap up this book, I want to leave you with something that shaped how I approach both business and teaching: the power of stories. Throughout this journey, I've shared real-life examples from my work in multifamily to show – not just tell – how success is built, mistake by mistake, win by win. Sometimes, advice can sound abstract. But stories – and especially case studies – bring it to life. While studying at Harvard Business School, we didn't just memorize frameworks; we learned by analyzing business case studies, many of them messy and incomplete. That's the reality of real estate. You rarely have every piece of information when negotiating a deal, especially in multi-family, where timing, market dynamics, and seller motivation all come into play.

I remember a deal where we had only a ten-day window to submit an offer on a 120-unit property in a rapidly appreciating submarket. The financials weren't fully clear, tenant turnover was high, and one building had known maintenance issues. But after reviewing the comps, analyzing nearby absorption rates, and understanding the potential rent lift through modest renovations, we made a calculated offer. It wasn't perfect – but it was informed. We secured the property, stabilized occupancy, and increased NOI by 22 percent in the first eighteen months. The takeaway? Success often lies in being decisive with the information you have – and refining the strategy as you go.

Theory and strategy are invaluable – but nothing compares to learning from real-world experience. Behind every successful real estate investor is a journey filled with triumphs, challenges, and hard-earned lessons. In this chapter, you'll meet a diverse group of investors who have navigated the complexities of multifamily investing – from first-time buyers to seasoned pros. Their stories reveal what works, what doesn't, and how mindset, persistence, and adaptability play crucial roles in turning opportunities into lasting success. These lessons from the field will inspire you, challenge your assumptions, and provide practical insights you can apply on your own path.

Real estate is a business of numbers – but it's also a business of people. Behind every deal is a story: a leap of faith, a calculated risk, a hard-won lesson. As much as we learn from theory and strategy, we learn just as much – if not more – from lived experience. From seeing what works, what doesn't, and what it actually takes to turn vision into results.

In this chapter, I want to introduce you to real investors – clients, colleagues, and peers – who've walked this path. Their stories are diverse, but they share one common thread: a commitment to growth, persistence, and purpose.

## Story #1: The First-Time Investor Who Turned Doubt Into Cash Flow

*"Doubt kills more dreams than failure ever will."*
— Suzy Kassem

Linda was a retired schoolteacher in her early sixties. She had spent her life in the classroom, guiding others toward their potential – yet when it came to her own financial future, she wasn't sure she had what it took.

"I'm not a businessperson," she told me during our first call. "I just want something simple. This will be my very first deal, therefore, I need something I can understand."

She had a modest pension, some savings in a retirement account, and a quiet but persistent dream of owning a rental property that could give her more financial freedom. But standing in her way wasn't money – it was doubt.

Together, we found a small triplex in a working-class neighborhood in Florida. It wasn't flashy, but it had strong bones, walkable amenities, and solid rental comps. Still, when the contractor opened up a bathroom wall and found unexpected water damage, Linda called me in a panic. "Did I just make a mistake?" she asked. "I don't know if I'm cut out for this."

We talked through it. The rehab budget had room for surprises, and her team was reliable. She didn't back down – and that decision became a turning point.

Six months later, the property was fully leased, professionally managed, and cash flowing. When she received her first full month of rent checks, she called me – not in panic, but in joy. "I can't believe this is working," she said. "This actually works."

Today, Linda is earning steady monthly income, she's refinanced to pull out capital, and she's already scouting her second property. She still doesn't think of herself as a "businessperson" – but she is, in the best sense: intentional, resilient, and quietly building her future.

Lesson: You don't need a business degree to succeed in real estate. You need courage, a plan, and the right people beside you when doubt creeps in. Linda didn't eliminate her fear – she moved forward anyway. And that's what made all the difference.

## Story #2: The High-Earner Who Discovered Passive Income Isn't Passive

*"Passive income isn't passive if you're constantly putting out fires."*
— Maria L. Ellis

Daniel was a successful corporate executive earning well into the six figures – but his multifamily investments were wearing him down. He had imagined mailbox money and weekend freedom. Instead, he found himself fielding tenant complaints during meetings, chasing contractors who ghosted him, and watching his so-called "passive income" consume every spare hour.

One evening, after missing his daughter's piano recital, he sat in his car exhausted and asked himself, *"Is this really worth it?"* That's when he called me.

One tenant stopped paying altogether. The other left in the middle of the night, taking more than just their furniture with them. The property manager changed twice in six months. Repairs piled up. Daniel called me with frustration in his voice: "This is more stressful than my day job. I wanted freedom, not another full-time responsibility."

We sat down and took a step back. What did he really want? What was his actual goal?

It wasn't about being hands-on. It was about building wealth without sacrificing peace of mind. Daniel didn't need to be the landlord – he needed to be the investor.

I introduced him to a multifamily syndication led by a seasoned team with a strong track record. This time, he invested as a limited partner. He contributed capital, received professional quarterly updates, and watched the returns come in – without late-night calls, contractor chaos, or eviction notices.

Today, Daniel is still a high-earner – but now, he's also a smart investor. His money is working in the background, aligned with his life instead of disrupting it.

Lesson: Passive income is only passive when it's structured intentionally. Sometimes the best move isn't to own and operate – it's to partner with those who do it well, so you can focus on what you do best.

## Story #3: The Value-Add Visionary Who Doubled Her Equity

*"Value isn't found – it's created by those who can see what others overlook."*
— Maria L. Ellis

Karen had spent years designing beautiful spaces for others. As a former architect, she knew how to transform buildings on paper   but she wanted to take it a step further: to **own** the transformation, not just draw it. Real estate investing, she believed, was her next chapter.

Still, the leap wasn't easy. She wondered if she was stepping too far outside her lane. *"What if I fail at something that's supposed to be my second act?"* she confided to a friend. Some colleagues warned her that investing was a completely different world – that passion wasn't enough without experience. But the pull was stronger than the fear. Karen moved forward, and what happened next proved that vision, backed by action is powerful. She found her canvas in a tired twelve-unit apartment building on the edge of a gentrifying neighborhood. The exterior was dated, the units were mismatched, and the property was poorly managed. Most investors had passed it over. But Karen saw more than peeling paint and below-market rents – she saw possibility.

With a mix of creativity and discipline, she got to work. She redesigned the interiors with cost-effective upgrades that elevated the space – modern flooring, smart lighting, fresh color schemes. She gave the facade a facelift and added thoughtful touches like improved signage and landscaping to increase curb appeal.

But her vision extended beyond aesthetics. She brought in a new property management team, reduced operating inefficiencies, and established clearer tenant communication. Rents were raised modestly – not aggressively – but occupancy increased because tenants recognized the improvements. The building went from overlooked to in-demand.

Two years later, the property was appraised at nearly double her purchase price. Karen executed a strategic refinance, pulling out tax-free equity she used to fund her next project – while still enjoying the improved cash flow from the first.

What started as a renovation became a transformation – not just of a building, but of Karen herself. She went from architect to investor, from planner to owner, and from earning fees to building lasting wealth.

Lesson: Value-add investing is about more than fixing what's broken. It's about vision, leadership, and operational precision. When you bring together design and discipline, you don't just renovate properties – you create equity from the ground up.

## Story #4: The Family That Built a Legacy – One Property at a Time

*"We didn't start with wealth – we started with a decision."*
— Maria L. Ellis

John and Maya were in their forties, juggling demanding careers, raising two teenagers, and doing everything "right" by conventional standards. They earned good salaries, paid their bills on time, and contributed to their retirement accounts. But despite all their effort, they felt like they were on a treadmill – always moving, never getting ahead.

One evening, after putting the kids to bed, John looked

across the table and said, "We're working so hard, but we're not building anything that lasts."

That moment became their turning point.

We sat down and created a ten-year plan that would transform their income into assets and their effort into legacy. Their first purchase wasn't flashy – a small four-unit property in a quiet, middle-income neighborhood. But it was theirs. They scraped together the down payment, took out a manageable loan, and made the leap.

What set John and Maya apart wasn't just their work ethic – it was their willingness to involve their children in the journey. I remember seeing their son helped paint the units on weekends. Their daughter created flyers for the available rentals and helped track income and expenses in a simple spreadsheet. Site visits became family outings, and dinner conversations shifted from school grades and chores to tenant issues, budgets, and goals.

This wasn't just real estate   it was a family project. A mission. A mindset shift.

As their confidence grew, so did their portfolio. They used equity from the first property to acquire a second, then a third. Each deal was more strategic, each step more intentional. But the greatest ROI wasn't financial – it was generational. Their kids didn't just hear about wealth-building; they lived it, one decision at a time.

Today, John and Maya are preparing to launch a family trust and plan to gift shares of their properties to their children as part of a long-term wealth strategy. But even more powerful than the assets are the conversations they've created – the mindset of ownership, stewardship, and possibility they've embedded in their family culture.

Lesson: Real estate isn't just about growing a portfolio – it's about growing people. When you involve your family in the process, you don't just build equity. You build legacy.

The stories you've just read aren't just anecdotes, they're proof that real estate investing is a journey shaped by decisions, resilience, and growth. Each investor faced unique challenges but found ways to adapt and thrive. Take their lessons to heart, apply what resonates, and remember: your story is still being written. With every step, you're building Your path to success, and with persistence

## My Invitation to You

These stories aren't meant to impress you, they're meant to inspire and ground you. Every investor faces uncertainty. Every project has its own speed bumps. But the difference between those who succeed and those who give up is not perfection – it's perseverance, resourcefulness, and vision.

No matter where you are on your journey, you have the ability to write your story. To take what you've learned, make your first (or next) move, and grow into the investor – and person – you were meant to become.

I've walked this road, too. I've made mistakes, taken risks, and learned through real-world experience what it means to lead with both strategy and heart. These stories reflect lessons I've lived and continue to learn. And now, I offer them to you – not as a blueprint, but as a reminder: you're not alone. The path forward is yours to shape.

## Clients' Stories, Real Lessons Checklist

### Collecting Client Stories

- Gather diverse stories covering different types of multifamily investments and challenges.
- Include examples of successes, setbacks, and lessons learned.
- Ensure stories highlight practical strategies and decision-making processes.

### Analyzing Key Themes

- Identify common challenges faced by clients (e.g., financing, tenant issues, market shifts).
- Extract actionable lessons and best practices from each story.

- Highlight innovative solutions and creative problem-solving approaches.

### *Applying Lessons Learned*

- Reflect on how each story's lessons relate to your own investment strategy.
- Develop plans to incorporate proven tactics into your operations.
- Avoid common pitfalls illustrated by client experiences.

### *Sharing and Learning*

- Use stories as case studies for team training and development.
- Encourage peer discussions and knowledge sharing within your network.
- Document ongoing client experiences to build a living resource for continuous learning.

### *Ethical Considerations*

- Obtain permission or anonymize details to protect client privacy.
- Present stories honestly, including both successes and failures.

## Reflection Questions

1. Which investor story in this chapter resonated most with you – and why?
2. What did you see in their journey that reflects Your hopes or challenges?
3. Have you ever doubted your ability to succeed in real estate?
4. What can you do to build your confidence and take the next step despite those doubts?
5. Do you prefer to be a hands-on investor like Karen, or a more passive participant like Daniel?
6. How can you align your strategy with your lifestyle and skillset?

7. Have you experienced a difficult or disappointing deal?
8. What lessons did you take from it that could help you avoid similar outcomes in the future?
9. What skills or experiences from your career or background can give you an edge as a real estate investor?
10. Are you involving your family in your investing journey?
11. If not, what's one small way you could start engaging them?
12. Which of the stories gave you a new idea or perspective to consider in Your investment strategy?
13. How do you typically react to setbacks in investing or business?
14. What mindset shift could help you stay focused during challenges?
15. Who do you know that might benefit from being included in your real estate journey – either as a partner, mentor, or mentee?
16. What will your real estate story look like one year from today if you take consistent action starting now?
17. Write out a short "future reflection" describing where you'll be, what you'll own, and how you'll feel.

# CHAPTER 22:
# EXIT STRATEGIES AND
# PORTFOLIO OPTIMIZATION

*"The best investment strategy isn't just knowing when to buy but mastering the art of when and how to exit."*

— Anonymous

In this chapter, I will teach you Exit Strategies and Portfolio Optimization, tailored to both beginner and intermediate investors. It will include practical guidance on when and how to sell, refinance, or exchange multifamily properties, as well as real-world case studies to illustrate each strategy in action. I'll let you know as soon as it's ready for your review.

Successful multifamily investment isn't just about acquiring properties; it's also about knowing how and when to exit those investments profitably. In real estate, an exit strategy is a plan for how you'll exit and profit.

For multifamily investors, having a well-defined exit plan from the outset is critical – it guides your decision-making during ownership and ensures you can capitalize on favorable market conditions when the time comes to divest.

This chapter will explore the major exit strategies available in multifamily real estate – including selling properties, refinancing, and executing 1031 exchanges – and discuss when and how to use each. We'll also examine the roles of market timing, tax implications, and portfolio optimization in crafting a successful exit. Real-world examples and case studies are included to illustrate how these strategies play out in practice, helping both beginner and intermediate investors understand the practical applications of each approach.

## Market Timing: Knowing When to Exit

Picture listing your building just as rents peak and buyers are bidding up prices. Timing your exit can significantly impact your investment's profitability. Real estate markets are cyclical, generally moving through phases of expansion (growth and rising values), peak, contraction (downturn), and recovery. A savvy investor aims to sell during a strong market or near the peak of a cycle, when buyer demand is high and pricing is most favorable. Selling during an upswing or expansion phase often means you can command a higher price, as cap rates (investment yields) tend to be low and buyers are willing to pay premiums for income-producing assets. By contrast, attempting to sell in a downturn or recessionary phase could result in lower offers and a longer time on market, as buyers become more cautious and values may stagnate or decline.

**Monitoring economic and market indicators** can help you identify these optimal windows. Monitoring economic and market indicators can help you identify these optimal windows. Factors like local job growth, population trends, rent growth, interest rate movements, and occupancy rates all signal the health of the multifamily market. For instance, low unemployment and rising rents often indicate a robust market, whereas increasing vacancy rates and flattening rents might foreshadow a slowdown. It's wise to keep an eye on broader economic indicators (GDP growth, interest rate changes) as well as local real estate data.

Take the case of a seventy-two-unit property we held in a fast-growing Sunbelt city. Over three years, we tracked consistent job growth, a population influx, and year-over-year rent increases. But then we noticed early signs of saturation – new construction was booming, and lease-up concessions were creeping in. At the same time, interest rates remained low, keeping buyer demand strong. Recognizing that the market was near its peak, we decided to list – and within weeks, sold at a premium to a buyer eager to enter the market. Had we waited another six months, rising vacancies and softening rents would likely have cut into our returns.

Market timing involves closely tracking such trends and indicators to pinpoint the best moment to sell, thereby maximizing returns by exiting during a favorable window.

In practice, you may not always hit the exact peak of the market (which is only evident in hindsight), but you can avoid obvious troughs and aim for a period when demand outpaces supply and pricing is strong. Remember, it's often better to sell a bit early in a hot market than too late in a declining one.

That said, perfect timing is difficult, and holding out for every last dollar of profit can be risky if market conditions shift. This is why your exit strategy should be formulated with a target timeline and return in mind, but also with some flexibility. Some investors set specific performance thresholds or market conditions that would trigger them to consider an exit (for example, if the property's value increases to a certain level, or if cap rates in the area compress below a given point). By planning ahead and staying attuned to market cycles, you can be proactive rather than reactive with your exits – positioning your property for sale when conditions are optimal, instead of being forced to sell during a downturn due to external pressures. In the next sections, we'll delve into specific exit strategies and how timing and preparation affect each one.

## Selling a Multifamily Property

Selling your multifamily property outright is the most straightforward exit strategy. In a traditional sale, you list the property on the market (often with the help of a commercial real estate broker), find a buyer, and transfer ownership in exchange for a lump sum payment. This approach provides complete liquidity and closure – you cash out your equity and end your involvement with the propertyloopnet.com. The key considerations when selling are when to sell (as discussed, aligning with market peaks if possible), how to prepare the asset for sale, and understanding the financial outcome including tax implications.

## When to Sell

Ideally, you choose to sell at a time when the property has achieved strong performance and when market conditions favor sellers. For example, many investors pursue a value-add strategy – they buy an underperforming apartment building, renovate units or improve management to increase rents and net operating income, then sell the property at a higher valuation once those improvements are realized. If the market is also on an upswing during this period, the investor can benefit doubly from the property's increased NOI and the market's higher pricing multiples.

Timing is crucial; selling during a strong real estate market can lead to higher sale price. Conversely, if local conditions change (say a major employer leaves town affecting demand, or new apartment supply floods the market), an investor might decide to sell sooner rather than later to avoid potential declines. Portfolio considerations also come into play – for instance, you might sell a property that has "peaked" in value or exhausted its upside, so you can redeploy that capital into new opportunities with more room for growth.

## How to Maximize Your Sale

Proper preparation can significantly impact your sale price and speed. Plan your exit well in advance – seasoned sellers often start getting a property ready for sale twelve to eighteen months ahead of listing. During this period, you'd want to address any deferred maintenance issues (to present a well-kept asset), stabilize occupancy at a high level (ideally above 90 percent with quality tenants), and continue to optimize operations to show increasing revenues. It's beneficial to compile a comprehensive due diligence package for prospective buyers, including at least two to three years of financial statements, rent rolls, maintenance and capital improvement records, and market comparables.

This documentation not only speeds up the transaction by instilling buyer confidence but also helps justify a premium price for your property. Engaging an experienced broker who specializes in multifamily properties can also add value – they can help with pricing strategy, marketing the asset to the right buyer pool (including other investors looking for turn-key rentals), and negotiating the best terms.

To illustrate the potential of a well-timed sale: Consider a real-world example of a multifamily investment purchased for $5 million in 2018. After targeted improvements, it was sold in 2020 for $8 million. During the two-year hold, the owners enjoyed steady cash flow – $105,000 in the first year and $135,000 in the second – while realizing a $3 million gain on sale. This kind of outcome, a 60 percent increase in value in just two years, was the result of a smart value-add strategy executed during a period of strong market appreciation. While such returns aren't guaranteed, the example shows how boosting a property's income and exiting at the right time can significantly maximize investment performance.

## Tax Implications of Selling

When you sell a multifamily property, you need to account for capital gains taxes on your profit, as well as depreciation recapture. Capital gains tax is applied to the difference between your sale price (minus selling costs) and your adjusted cost basis in the property. If you've held the property for more than one year, you qualify for long-term capital gains tax rates (typically 15 percent or 20 percent at the federal level, depending on your income bracket, plus any state taxes). Depreciation recapture is a critical but sometimes overlooked aspect – over the course of ownership, you likely depreciated the property and took those deductions to reduce taxable income.

Upon sale, the IRS wants to "recapture" those tax benefits: any gain attributable to depreciation is taxed at a special depreciation recapture rate (the unrecaptured Section1250 gain) of up to 25 percent. In simple terms, if you claimed $200,000 worth of depreciation during ownership, that portion of your gain will be taxed at 25 percent (you will owe up to $50,000 in this example), even if your remaining gain might be taxed at the lower capital gains rate. The combination of capital gains and depreciation recapture can take a significant bite out of your sale proceeds – easily 20 to 30 percent or more of your profit can go to taxes.

Because of this, investors often seek ways to minimize or defer taxes when selling. One straightforward (though not always pleasant) method is to offset gains with losses – for example, selling another investment at a loss in the same year to offset the multifamily gain, or using carryover losses from other activities. However, the most powerful tool real estate investors use to defer taxes is the 1031 exchange, which we will cover shortly. It's worth noting here that if you choose not to (or cannot) do a 1031 exchange upon sale, you should set aside funds for the tax liabilities or consult with a CPA for strategies to mitigate the impact.

Sometimes, investors are prepared to pay the tax because they want to cash out and perhaps use the funds outside of real estate; other times, paying the tax might be acceptable if the post-tax profit still meets their goals. The key is to plan ahead for taxes as part of your exit – there's nothing worse than being caught by surprise by a large tax bill after you've already reinvested or spent the proceeds.

What will you do with the money once the income stream is gone?" You'll want to ensure you have good use for the sales proceeds, whether it's another investment, paying down debt elsewhere, or some other purpose, so that your money continues to work for you. On the positive side, selling frees up your capital, which can then be reinvested in new opportunities or used to diversify your portfolio into different markets or asset types. If you've made a healthy profit, selling can also substantially boost your liquidity and net worth, giving you dry powder for the next deal. In summary, selling is a clean exit that, when timed and executed well, locks in your gains and allows you to reposition your portfolio – just go in with a solid plan for taxes and reinvestment to maximize the benefit.

## Refinancing as a Strategy: "Exit" Without Selling

Not every exit involves selling the property outright. Refinancing your multifamily property is an alternative exit strategy that lets you unlock the equity you've built without giving up ownership. In essence, a refinance entails replacing your original mortgage with a new loan – often one that is larger (if the property value has gone up) or on better terms (such as a lower interest rate or longer amortization period). By doing so, you can pull out cash from the property's increased equity or improve the property's cash flow by reducing debt service. This strategy is sometimes referred to as a "cash-out refinance and hold," and it functions as a partial exit: you are exiting your original financing position and possibly taking some profit off the table, but you *continue to hold the asset* and benefit from future income and appreciation.

## When and Why to Refinance

A refinance is most attractive after your property has appreciated in value or after you have significantly increased its net operating income (through improvements or better management). For example, suppose you purchased an apartment complex, improved the units and raised rents, and as a result the property's value jumped from $1 million to $1.5 million. You could refinance into a new mortgage that reflects this higher value – lenders might allow, say, a 75 percent loan-to-value (LTV) loan, which on a $1.5 million valuation is $1.125 million. Refinancing to that amount would first pay off your remaining old loan balance, and the surplus would be cashed out to you at closing. This effectively lets you extract some (or all) of your original investment.

In many cases, investors use a cash-out refinance to recapture their initial down payment and renovation expenses, essentially putting them in a position of having "no money left in the deal." For instance, one investor was able to do exactly that: after renovating a ninety-unit apartment property and increasing its value, he refinanced and pulled out his entire down payment and rehab costs – recouping his initial capital – while still retaining ownership of the property. At that point, any further cash flow or future sale proceeds from the property would be pure profit, since his original capital was back in his pocket. With that capital in hand, most investors either diversify into new markets or scale their portfolio by acquiring larger or more profitable assets – effectively accelerating their growth without injecting new money.

Refinancing can also be driven by interest rate conditions. If interest rates have fallen significantly since you took out your original loan, refinancing might reduce your monthly mortgage payments and increase cash flow. Even if you don't take cash out, moving from, say, a 5.5 percent interest rate to a 4 percent rate (or from an interest-only bridge loan to a long-term fixed-rate loan) can save thousands of dollars a month in debt service. This can make the deal far more sustainable long-term.

On the flip side, be cautious about refinancing in a high interest rate environment. Pulling out equity at a significantly higher rate can shrink your cash flow and increase financial risk. That's why every refinance decision should include a careful analysis of your **Debt Service Coverage Ratio (DSCR)** – a key metric that compares a property's net operating income (NOI) to its debt obligations.

A **healthy DSCR** is typically 1.25 or higher, meaning the property generates 25 percent more income than it needs to cover its debt payments. For example, if a property has $125,000 in NOI and $100,000 in annual debt service, the DSCR is 1.25 – comfortably covering the loan with a buffer for vacancies or unexpected expenses.

An **unhealthy DSCR**, on the other hand, might look like 1.05 or lower – indicating that the property barely covers its debt, with little margin for error. Refinancing under those conditions can leave you vulnerable to shifts in occupancy, rent declines, or rising expenses.

Seasoned investors wait for the right moment: when property value has increased, interest rates are reasonable, and income levels are strong enough to support a larger loan **while maintaining a safe DSCR**. That's how you protect your upside while managing your downside.

## Benefits of Refinancing

The chief benefit is that you get to access your equity without selling, meaning you don't trigger capital gains taxes at that point. The cash you receive from a refinance is essentially loan proceeds – not taxable income – so it is a way to pull out "tax-free" money from your investment (it's tax-free now because it's debt, though of course the debt must be paid back over time). This can be a powerful way to fund new investments and grow your portfolio. By securing a new loan with better terms, investors can tap into equity to finance other acquisitions or improvements, effectively allowing them to diversify or expand their portfolio without selling the current asset. For example, you might refinance one apartment building and use the cash to help with the down payment on another, thereby turning one asset into two. Many investors use the refinance-and-hold strategy to scale up – it's akin to the BRRRR method (Buy, Rehab, Rent, Refinance, Repeat) used often in residential investing, applied to multifamily properties.

Another benefit is that you retain ownership of the property, so you continue to collect rental income and can potentially benefit from further appreciation. You're essentially taking some chips off the table (in the form of equity cashed out) while still riding the growth of the asset. This is why refinancing can be described as having the *"best of both worlds" – you get liquidity now while keeping future upside*. If you believe strongly in the property's long-term prospects, or if selling would leave you with the challenge of finding a comparable investment in a tight market, refinancing to hold can be attractive.

## Risks and Considerations

Refinancing – especially with a cash-out component – typically increases your debt load and monthly payments. While this can unlock capital for new investments, it also reduces your cash flow cushion and raises your exposure to risk. You're essentially **re-leveraging** the property, and more leverage means greater sensitivity to vacancies, rising expenses, or economic downturns.

One common mistake is pulling out so much equity that the property's cash flow barely covers the new mortgage. This leaves you with a thin margin for error and a weak **Debt Service Coverage Ratio (DSCR)**, making it difficult to weather short-term disruptions.

Higher leverage can also limit your exit options. If market conditions soften, a highly-leveraged property may be harder to sell at a profit or refinance again without injecting new capital.

Smart investors always stress-test the deal. Run scenarios like: *What if occupancy drops by 10 percent? What if operating costs rise? What if I'm on a variable-rate loan and rates go up?* If the numbers still work under pressure, you're in a safer position to move forward.

Transaction costs for refinancing (closing costs, loan fees, etc.) can be significant, so factor those in when determining if a refi makes financial sense. Sometimes, if the amount of cash you can pull out is small, it may not be worth the effort and cost. Additionally, if you have a prepayment penalty or yield maintenance on the existing loan, that could eat into the benefit of refinancing. Check your current loan terms.

It's also worth timing a refinance with market conditions: in a high-interest rate environment, you might delay refinancing (unless you're forced due to loan maturity) and instead use that time to improve property value, then refinance when rates improve. Some investors proactively refinance before a loan's term is up (even if there's a small penalty) because they fear interest rates might climb in the future – locking in a decent rate now could save money in the long run. For instance, during 2023 some multifamily owners refinanced earlier than planned to secure fixed interest rates, anticipating that borrowing costs would rise.

In summary, refinancing can be an excellent strategy to optimize your portfolio's capital structure. It's about unlocking your equity without giving up the asset. A successful refinance can enhance your overall returns: you get to reinvest the pulled-out equity elsewhere (potentially earning returns in two places), and you still have the original property working for you. Just use this tool judiciously – avoid the temptation to over-leverage, and ensure that any refinanced debt aligns with your long-term investment horizon (e.g., don't put short-term high-interest debt on a property you intend to hold for many years without a plan to address it). Many experienced investors will tell you that real estate is a game of finance as much as bricks and mortar – mastering the refinance strategy is a key part of that game.

## 1031 Exchanges: Deferring Taxes and Trading Up

One of the most powerful exit strategies in real estate, particularly for those looking to continually grow their portfolio, is the 1031 exchange. Named after Section 1031 of the U.S. Internal Revenue Code, this strategy allows you to sell one investment property and buy another "like-kind" property while deferring capital gains taxes on the sale. It's essentially a tax strategy for "trading up" your assets. Many investors use 1031 exchanges to move from a smaller property to a larger one, or from a less desirable asset to a more desirable one, without getting hit immediately with taxes that could erode their investable equity.

## How a 1031 Exchange Works

When you sell your multifamily property, instead of taking the proceeds into Your account, the cash goes to a qualified intermediary (an independent third party who facilitates the exchange). You then direct that intermediary to use the funds to purchase another investment property that qualifies as "like-kind." *Like-kind* in real estate is quite broad – essentially any other real property held for investment will qualify (for example, you can sell an apartment building and buy another apartment building, a portfolio of rental houses, a retail center, or a piece of land, as long as it's investment real estate).

By doing this exchange, the IRS allows you to defer paying the capital gains and depreciation recapture taxes that would normally be due on the sale. It's not a tax forgiveness – it's a deferral, meaning the gain carries into the new property. But you can keep deferring indefinitely by doing successive 1031 exchanges each time you sell a property, effectively kicking the tax can down the road. In fact, if you never "cash out" and eventually pass away holding the property, your heirs may receive a step-up in basis, potentially avoiding those deferred taxes entirely.

To qualify for a 1031 exchange, there are strict timing and process rules you must follow. As soon as you close the sale of your relinquished property, the clock starts ticking. Within forty-five days, you must formally identify in writing the potential replacement property (or properties) you intend to buy. You can generally identify up to three properties (or more under certain valuation rules) as candidates, in case one deal falls through. Then, you must complete the purchase of at least one of those identified properties within 180 days from the sale of the original property. These deadlines are inflexible – missing them would disqualify the exchange and result in your sale being fully taxable.

Additionally, the total purchase price of the replacement property (or combined prices of multiple replacements) typically needs to be equal to or greater than the sale price of the relinquished property, and you must reinvest all of the cash proceeds (if you keep some cash, that portion is taxable as "boot"). Another requirement is that you use a Qualified Intermediary (QI) to handle the funds – you, as the investor, cannot take possession of the sale proceeds at any point, or the IRS will consider it a taxable receipt. The QI holds the money and applies it toward the new purchase to maintain the exchange's integrity.

Because of these rules, it's important to plan your 1031 exchange in advance. Ideally, you should start looking for suitable replacement properties *before* you sell the current one, or at least have a clear idea of what you'll exchange into. In a hot market, forty-five days can pass quickly, and finding the right deal under pressure can be challenging. Some investors even negotiate a longer closing period on their sale, or use extension strategies like a *reverse 1031 exchange* (where you buy the replacement property before selling the original, using a special structure) if they need more flexibility. Professional guidance from a QI and a tax advisor is highly recommended when doing a 1031, especially for the first time.

## Why Use a 1031 Exchange

The primary benefit is tax deferral. By avoiding capital gains tax – often around 20 percent – and depreciation recapture tax – typically 25 percent – you retain significantly more equity to roll into your next investment. This can dramatically accelerate portfolio growth. A 1031 exchange allows you to preserve your investment capital and leverage it into a larger or better-performing asset, instead of handing a substantial portion over to the government.

For example, imagine you bought a multifamily property for $1 million, and it's now worth $1.8 million. If you sold it outright, the $800,000 gain could generate approximately $200,000 in taxes (depending on depreciation and your tax bracket), leaving you with $600,000 to reinvest. But through a 1031 exchange, you can roll the full $800,000 gain – plus your original $1 million basis – into the next deal. Over time, this difference is enormous. That's why 1031 exchanges are often called one of the most powerful wealth-building tools in real estate. You're essentially using deferred tax dollars – *the government's money* – to grow your investment portfolio.

Another reason investors use 1031 exchanges is to "trade up" or optimize their holdings. You might start with a small four-unit building and through a 1031 exchange move into a twelve-unit property, then later exchange into a fifty-unit, and so on. Each step, your portfolio grows in size and potentially in the quality of asset. By using 1031 exchanges, investors can preserve their gains and continually upgrade to larger or higher-income properties. Similarly, you can exchange into a property that better fits your current investment goals – for instance, trading a older property with lots of maintenance issues for a newer building with lower operating costs, or moving from a slow-growth market to a high-growth market, all while deferring taxes. It's also a way to rearrange your portfolio mix: some investors use 1031s to consolidate (selling two smaller properties to buy one larger one) or to diversify (selling one big property to buy several smaller ones in different locations). One real-life case study highlighted how an investor went from a duplex to a twelve-unit apartment via a 1031 exchange, significantly boosting cash flow and portfolio size without incurring immediate tax on the transition.

Let's look at a concrete example of the impact: *In one scenario, an investor sold a multifamily* property and deferred approximately $200,000 in capital gains taxes by executing a 1031 exchange into a larger multifamily asset. By not paying that $200,000 to the IRS, the investor had that much more equity available to invest in the new property, which not only increased their potential cash flow but also positioned them for greater long-term appreciation on a more valuable asset. Essentially, the investor turned what would have been a tax payment into additional real estate investment – a move that accelerated their wealth-building. Moreover, 1031 exchanges can be repeated. Many savvy investors rinse and repeat this strategy, compounding their growth as they roll from one property to the next, all the while deferring taxes. (And if one wants to eventually cash out and pay taxes, they can – ideally at a time or in a manner that is most tax-efficient, or never if their plan is to hold until estate settlement.)

## Things to Watch Out For

While powerful, 1031 exchanges are not without challenges. The tight identification and closing windows can create pressure and potentially lead to suboptimal acquisitions if you're not careful – Don't let the 45/180-day clock push you into a bad deal. It's crucial to maintain discipline and have backup options identified. The properties must be genuinely like-kind and held for investment (you cannot 1031 exchange your personal residence, for example, nor flip a property you held just a few months as inventory). If an exchange fails (e.g., you miss the deadline or the deal falls apart outside the window), you'll end up owing the full taxes from the sale, so timing and execution are everything. Due diligence on the replacement property is still paramount; a 1031 doesn't make a bad deal good, it just defers taxes.

Also remember that a 1031 is a deferral, not a permanent exclusion (unless you employ other strategies later). If you eventually sell without doing another exchange, you'll owe taxes on the cumulative gains and depreciation from all the previous properties. Some investors plan a final exit via estate planning – if the property goes to heirs, the basis can step up, effectively wiping out the deferred gain. Others might eventually "cash out" in a year where they have offsetting losses or in a low-income year to reduce the tax hit. There are also scenarios like partial 1031 exchanges (where you don't reinvest everything – you can do that, you'll just pay tax on the portion not reinvested) and DSTs (Delaware Statutory Trusts) which allow exchange into fractional ownership of large properties for more passive investment – those are advanced topics beyond the scope here, but worth noting as part of the exit strategy lexicon.

In summary, a 1031 exchange is a cornerstone strategy for serious real estate investors focused on long-term portfolio growth and tax efficiency. By deferring taxes, you keep more of your money working for you. By carefully selecting your replacement properties, you can continually improve your portfolio's value and performance. The process requires planning, but the reward is the ability to build wealth exponentially – as one might say, it's not just what you make on a deal, but what you keep, and a 1031 helps you keep the gains rolling forward.

## Other Exit Strategies to Consider

While selling, refinancing, and 1031 exchanges are among the most common exit paths, there are several other strategies and variations that multifamily investors might employ as part of their exit and portfolio optimization plan. Savvy investors sometimes use lesser-known (but powerful) alternatives like these.

### Condo Conversion

This involves taking a multifamily rental property (say a ten-unit apartment building) and legally converting it into individual condominium units that can be sold separately. In certain markets, the sum of selling units one-by-one can exceed the price of selling the building as a whole. *By turning an apartment building into condos, an investor can* often sell each unit at a higher per-unit price, thereby *maximizing total profit.* This strategy also allows for flexibility – you could sell the condos gradually, timing sales with market conditions, rather than one bulk sale. However, conversion comes with legal and logistical complexity (you'll need to get a condo map recorded, possibly upgrade systems to meet condo regulations, etc.), and it works best in markets where there's strong demand from individual condo buyers (often urban areas with high home prices). It's an advanced strategy, but one that has been successfully used to "exit" a multifamily investment by effectively turning it into a series of smaller sales.

### Seller Financing (Owner Financing)

In a seller-financing exit, you *sell the property to a buyer but you become the bank* for some or all of the purchase price. Instead of traditional financing, the buyer pays you directly over time – with interest. The benefit to you as the seller is that you can often get a quicker sale or a higher price (your financing is part of the value to the buyer), and you earn interest income on the loan you've given. It can also spread out your capital gains over time (potentially using the installment sale tax method). This strategy essentially provides a steady *income stream after sale, as you receive regular* mortgage payments from the buyer (with interest). The downside is you still carry risk: if the buyer defaults, you may have to foreclose and take the property back. You also don't get all your cash out at once (which might limit immediate reinvestment, unless you sell the note). Seller financing is typically used when you own the property free and clear (or can pay off any mortgage at closing) and is more common in smaller deals or when the buyer has trouble getting conventional financing. It's an option to keep the cash flow coming even after "selling," but be sure you vet the buyer's credit and have a solid loan agreement in place.

### Partial Sale or Partnership Buyout

Not every exit is all-or-nothing. If you co-own a property with partners, one exit route could be to sell your share to your partner or another investor. Alternatively, you might bring in a new partner who buys a portion of your equity, giving you partial liquidity. This can happen in syndications or joint ventures where, say, one investor wants to cash out while others prefer to continue holding. Such a partial exit allows an investor to take some profit off the table while a new or remaining investor takes on that *stake*.

For example, imagine you and a partner own a multi-family property worth $4 million, and your share is valued at $2 million. Instead of selling your entire interest, you could sell half of your stake – $1 million worth – to a new investor. You pocket that $1 million while still holding a $1 million interest in the property. This kind of partial exit is common in syndications or joint ventures, especially when one investor wants to cash out while others prefer to continue holding. It requires careful valuation and clear terms, but it can be an effective way to rebalance your portfolio, free up capital, and avoid a full sale that could trigger taxes or disrupt the investment's long-term strategy.

### *"Hold Forever" and Estate Planning*

On the flip side from selling, some investors plan to hold long-term, even indefinitely, as part of a legacy or estate plan. The "exit" in this case is not a sale during the investor's lifetime but rather passing the property on to heirs or beneficiaries. The advantage here is that if structured properly, you can minimize taxes through strategies like the stepped-up basis at death (where heirs receive the property with the tax basis reset to market value, potentially erasing the capital gain). This approach focuses on generational wealth and ongoing cash flow – the property might continue to throw off income for the family trust or heirs, instead of being liquidated. However, it requires thinking through management succession (who will manage the property) or whether eventually the heirs will sell (at which point the stepped-up basis would eliminate past gains for tax purposes). Even if you intend to hold long-term, it's prudent to periodically review if that still makes sense – sometimes market conditions or family needs change. But for some, the plan is to *never sell*, effectively using refinances and estate planning as the "exit" to pull equity as needed and then transfer wealth to the next generation.

Each of these strategies has its own benefits and pitfalls, and they may or may not align with your goals. Beginners might not utilize the more complex options like condo conversions right away, but it's good to be aware of them as your experience grows. Intermediate investors might have situations where a hybrid or creative exit unlocks value— for example, a partnership restructuring or a seller financing deal to get a tough sale done. The common thread is that flexibility and creativity can sometimes solve problems or open up opportunities that the primary strategies (sale, refi, 1031) don't address. Always weigh the complexity and risk against the rewards. In many cases, these alternatives are executed with the help of professionals (attorneys, accountants, and consultants) to ensure they're done correctly.

## Aligning Exit Strategies with Portfolio Optimization

Choosing an exit strategy is not a one-size-fits-all decision – it should be closely aligned with your overall portfolio goals and investment strategy. As a multifamily investor, you'll likely own multiple properties over time (or simultaneously), and how you exit one investment can have a cascading effect on your ability to grow or stabilize your portfolio. This section looks at how to integrate exit planning into your broader portfolio management to achieve optimal results.

### *Start with Your Investment Goals*

Are you aiming for maximum growth, steady cash flow, or a balance of both? Your answer will influence your exits. If your goal is aggressive growth and portfolio expansion, you might favor strategies like 1031 exchanges or cash-out refinances that allow you to roll equity forward into new acquisitions. For example, an investor who starts with a small apartment building might use a refinance to pull out equity (as we saw with the earlier case study) and then use those funds to acquire a second property, thereby doubling the portfolio without an outright sale. Later, that investor might sell one property and 1031 exchange into an even larger asset, continuing to scale up. In one illustrative case, an investor purchased a ninety-unit property for around $3 million and over a few years increased its value. He refinanced to recapture his initial capital, then ultimately put the property under contract to sell for $4.9 million, planning to execute a 1031 exchange into a higher-class multifamily or larger asset. This series of moves – value-add, refinance, then sell and exchange – allowed him to grow from one apartment building into a more valuable portfolio, all while deferring taxes and optimizing the use of equity. The strategy was dictated by a clear growth goal.

If your primary goal is passive income and a long-term hold, you might choose to refinance for better cash flow – such as securing a lower interest rate – or bring in partners to reduce your workload without giving up ownership entirely. In some cases, it makes sense to sell only the properties that no longer meet your cash flow targets while holding onto stronger performers.

### *Regular Portfolio Review – "Optimize or Exit"*

Savvy investors periodically review each asset in their portfolio to decide if it still fits or if your equity is sitting idle and could be working harder in another asset.

An apartment building that was a great buy ten years ago might now have, say, 70 percent of its value sitting in equity due to loan paydown and appreciation – but perhaps its rent yield on that equity has become low. In such a case, you might consider exiting that investment (through sale or refi) to redeploy the equity into new projects with higher returns. For instance, suppose Property A has grown in value and now the return on the current equity is only 5 percent, whereas you could move that equity into Property B or C that would yield 8 to 10 percent. By selling or refinancing Property A, you can rebalance your portfolio for higher overall returns. This decision-making process is part of portfolio optimization: continuously evaluating if each dollar of equity is working as hard as possible. If not, an exit strategy is the mechanism to move that dollar to a better opportunity.

Portfolio reviews should also consider diversification and risk. You might find that you're overexposed in one geographic market or too heavily weighted in one asset class. Exiting one or two properties and reallocating capital into different markets can reduce risk. One investor, for example, used a 1031 exchange to diversify their holdings across different cities, selling a property in one market to acquire properties in two new markets, thereby spreading geographic risk while still deferring taxes. Another scenario: if you anticipate an economic downturn or interest rate spike, you might opt to sell a highly leveraged or marginally performing property to de-risk your portfolio, even if the timing isn't ideal from a market standpoint. It's about the bigger picture of what makes your entire portfolio stronger.

### *Tax Strategy and Coordination*

From a portfolio perspective, you can also strategize exits in a way that manages tax impacts year to year. If you have multiple properties, you might stagger sales and exchanges to avoid a huge tax hit all in one year. Or, if you generate a large paper loss (perhaps through depreciation or a cost segregation study on a new acquisition), that might be an opportune time to sell another property and use that loss to offset the gain. A well-optimized portfolio takes into account that taxes, like any other cost, drag on returns – so planning exits with tax efficiency (such as utilizing 1031 exchanges or timing sales with other tax events) will improve your net outcomes. High-net-worth investors often have tax advisors run projections on various sell versus hold scenarios across their portfolio to decide which exit to do when.

### *4. Flexibility and Contingency Plans*

We've stressed planning, but it's worth repeating that staying flexible is crucial. Market conditions can change unexpectedly, and personal circumstances can evolve (maybe you want to retire earlier, or you need liquidity for a non-real-estate opportunity, etc.). A smart portfolio optimization approach includes contingency exit plans. For example, you might plan to hold Property X long-term, but you also have a price in mind at which you would sell if the market offered it. Or you might be ready to pivot an attempted 1031 exchange into just selling and paying tax if you can't find a suitable replacement (sometimes paying the tax and holding cash for the next deal is better than buying a poor asset just to defer tax). In your mind (or better, in a written plan), outline alternative exits for each asset: "If plan A (say, refi next year) doesn't work due to rates or lender constraints, plan B might be to sell and 1031, or plan C to hold longer until market improves," etc. Being prepared with multiple strategies ensures you're not caught flat-footed. As one industry saying goes, "Invest with a plan, but adapt as needed."

### *5. The Human Factor – Time and Effort*

Portfolio optimization isn't solely about the numbers; it's also about your personal bandwidth and lifestyle goals. Managing a portfolio of multifamily properties can be demanding. You might reach a point where simplifying is part of optimization – for instance, streamlining by consolidating multiple smaller properties into a single, more manageable asset. Or perhaps transitioning from active ownership to a more passive role (through vehicles like syndications or real estate funds) becomes appealing; in that case, your exit strategy might involve selling your assets and moving capital into passive investments for the sake of time freedom. Therefore, the "optimal" portfolio is not just the one with the highest theoretical return, but the one that best balances risk, return, and the investor's capacity and preference for involvement.

By aligning each exit decision with these broader considerations, you effectively turn exit strategy into a portfolio management tool. Instead of viewing an exit as the end of an investment, see it as a pivot point – an opportunity to enhance your position and move closer to your financial objectives. Whether you are a beginner planning the future path of a first four-plex, or an intermediate investor juggling several apartment buildings, this integrated perspective will help ensure that each property's lifecycle (buy, hold, exit) contributes to your overall financial success.

## Conclusion

Planning your exit is just as important as planning your purchase in multifamily real estate investing. A well-crafted exit strategy not only maximizes the returns on the deal at hand, but also positions you for greater opportunities and wealth accumulation down the line. We've discussed the primary exit routes – selling, refinancing, and 1031 exchanges – along with variations and examples of each. By now, you should understand *when and how* to use these strategies: Sell when the timing and asset's performance align for a profitable cash-out (and prepare meticulously to get top dollar); refinance when you want to retain a good asset but harvest equity or improve terms; execute a 1031 exchange when you aim to grow or reposition your portfolio without losing a big chunk of gains to taxes. We also touched on alternative exits like condo conversions, partial sales, or holding for legacy, which might play a role as your portfolio evolves.

A few key takeaways to remember:

Always begin with the end in mind: Before you even buy a property, consider your likely exit strategy and timeframe. This will guide your business plan (for example, how you renovate or how you finance the deal) and set expectations for your investors or partners. As the saying goes, *you make your money in real estate when you buy, but you realize that money when you sell.*

Market cycles matter: Keep an eye on the economic climate and local real estate trends. While you can't time the market perfectly, being roughly right is better than precisely wrong. Aim to exit in favorable conditions and avoid being a forced seller in a down market. Use data – vacancy rates, rent growth, interest rates, etc. – to inform your decisions on timing.

Maximize value before exit: Whether selling or refinancing, boost your property's performance ahead of the event. Increase your NOI, tidy up physical and financial due diligence items, and make the asset as attractive as possible. This preparation can significantly improve the outcome, as demonstrated by successful investors who list properties with strong occupancy, clean financials, and documented improvements to justify premium pricing.

Consider taxes and reinvestment: Calculate the tax impacts of a sale and weigh options like the 1031 exchange. Sometimes the best move is to defer taxes and keep capital working; other times, it might make sense to pay the tax and enjoy the freedom of cash (or diversify into stocks, etc.). What's crucial is that you *consciously decide* and incorporate tax planning rather than stumble into a tax bill. If you do cash out, have a plan for those proceeds – idle cash can erode returns, so know your next move (even if that move is paying off debt or another financial goal).

Stay flexible: Markets change, and so do personal circumstances. A strategy that looked good five years ago might need adjustment. Be willing to pivot – for instance, if interest rates skyrocket, maybe your planned refinance becomes unfeasible and selling (or holding longer) is better. Or if the market is red-hot, you might sell sooner than intended to seize the opportunity. As one multifamily COO noted, it's essential to have a plan but equally important to *be flexible*, adapting your strategy as needed when life and markets throw curveballs.

Learn from experience and others: Each deal you go through will teach you something about exits. Maybe you sold one property too early and left money on the table, or maybe you held one too long. Take those lessons forward. Also, pay attention to case studies and stories from other investors – real-world examples (like those we shared) highlight what's possible and what pitfalls to avoid. Don't hesitate to seek advice from mentors, brokers, or financial advisors when plotting a complex exit.

In closing, exit strategies and portfolio optimization go hand in hand. A single multifamily property can be transformed through strategic exits into a ladder that climbs you up to greater investments, or it can be a cash cow you hold for income – or even a legacy you pass on. By understanding the tools at your disposal, timing your moves, and integrating your exit approach with your overall investment plan, you set yourself up to "stick the landing" of each investment. This way, you're not just investing in real estate, you're building wealth intelligently, always planning a few moves ahead (like a good chess game, as the analogy goes. Whether you're just starting out or looking to level up your portfolio, keep your exit strategy clear, your execution nimble, and your eyes on the prize of long-term financial success in the multifamily game. Happy investing, and may your exits be as rewarding as your entries!

## Exit Strategies and Portfolio Optimization Checklist

### Goal Setting and Planning

- Define your short-term and long-term exit objectives.
- Establish financial benchmarks that trigger exit consideration (e.g., target IRR, property value).
- Integrate exit planning into your overall investment strategy from acquisition onward.

### Market Analysis and Timing

- Regularly monitor local market conditions and economic indicators.

- Assess property performance against market rent and vacancy trends.
- Evaluate timing relative to real estate cycles and interest rate environments.

### Sale Preparation

- Conduct thorough property inspections and complete necessary repairs.
- Stabilize occupancy and tenant quality prior to listing.
- Prepare comprehensive due diligence packages for prospective buyers.
- Engage an experienced broker specializing in multifamily assets.

### Refinancing Considerations

- Review current loan terms and potential refinancing benefits.
- Calculate expected cash-out amounts and impacts on cash flow.
- Analyze refinancing costs, fees, and potential interest rate changes.

### Tax Planning

- Consult with tax professionals regarding capital gains, depreciation recapture, and 1031 exchanges.
- Plan and execute 1031 exchanges if applicable to defer taxes.
- Understand implications of various exit strategies on your tax position.

### Portfolio Review and Optimization

- Perform regular portfolio assessments to identify underperforming or non-core assets.
- Consider diversification strategies to reduce risk and enhance returns.

- Align asset disposition or acquisition decisions with evolving investment goals.

## *Execution*

- Finalize legal documents and disclosures for sale or refinancing.
- Coordinate timing with lenders, buyers, and investors.
- Communicate exit plans transparently with all stakeholders.
- Close transactions efficiently and ensure proper transfer of funds and responsibilities.

## Reflection Questions

1. What are your primary goals for your multifamily investments in the next five to ten years?
2. How do these goals influence your preferred exit strategies?
3. How well do you understand the current market cycle and local economic indicators?
4. Are you monitoring trends that affect the timing of your exits?
5. Have you identified potential triggers or benchmarks (e.g., property value, cap rate, cash flow) that would signal it's time to sell or refinance?
6. What are the tax implications of selling your properties, and how comfortable are you with strategies like 1031 exchanges to defer taxes?
7. Have you planned for alternative exit strategies if your preferred option becomes impractical (e.g., market downturn, financing changes)?
8. How do you evaluate whether refinancing is a better option than selling in a given market environment?
9. Do you have a clear process for preparing properties for sale to maximize value and attract buyers?
10. How often do you conduct portfolio reviews to

assess which properties to hold, refinance, or exit?

11. Are you leveraging partnerships, advisors, and professionals effectively to optimize your exit strategies?

12. What steps can you take today to improve your readiness and flexibility for executing your next exit or portfolio optimization move?

# CHAPTER 23:
# YOUR ROAD MAP FORWARD

*"The best way to predict the future is to create it."*
— Peter Drucker

You've journeyed through the fundamentals, strategies, and stories of multifamily real estate investing. Now it's time to translate knowledge into action. Success isn't just about what you know – it's about how you apply it consistently over time.

In this final chapter, we'll pull everything together into a clear, actionable road map. Whether you're just starting out or looking to scale, this guide will help you set priorities, build momentum, and stay focused on the goals that matter most. Your future as a confident, purposeful investor begins with the steps you take today.

You've made it to the end of this book – but your journey as a real estate investor is just beginning.

By now, you've gained a deep understanding of real estate investing – from defining your identity and analyzing deals to building your team, leveraging financing, harnessing technology, and creating a legacy. You've also read real stories of investors just like you – people who started with uncertainty and turned it into ownership, impact, and freedom.

Let's figure out what happens next.

Whether you are brand new to investing or already own properties, the path forward starts with a simple truth:

Clarity + Commitment + Consistent Action = Progress.

## Step 1: Reconnect with Your Why

Before making your next move, it's essential to reconnect with your why – the deeper reason you started investing in the first place. Your "why" serves as your compass, guiding every decision, keeping you focused through uncertainty, and ensuring that your strategy aligns with the life you truly want to build.

What motivated you to explore real estate in the first place?

Was it…

- The desire for passive income?
- The dream of financial freedom?
- A way to leave something meaningful behind?
- The need to escape burnout, stagnation, or financial pressure?

Write it down. Post it somewhere visible. Your "why" is your anchor. It will guide your decisions, steady you during setbacks, and remind you of what really matters.

## Step 2: Choose Your Investment Strategy

Based on what you've learned, what kind of investor are you?

- Active or passive?
- Residential or multifamily?
- Local or out-of-state?
- Cash flow focused or value-add driven?

Define your buy box. Know your comfort zone – but be willing to stretch it as you gain experience.

## Step 3: Build or Strengthen Your Team

Surround yourself with professionals who share your values, respect your vision, and bring complementary skills. Don't go it alone – relationships are your most valuable resource.

If you're just starting, begin by connecting with a trusted broker, lender, or investor-friendly attorney. One relationship can change everything.

## Step 4: Build Your Ninety-Day Action Plan

Break your big goals into clear, manageable steps you can take over the next ninety days. Focus on progress, not perfection.

You don't need all the answers – just a place to start.

Don't aim to build an empire overnight. Focus on traction.

What can you commit to in the next ninety days?

- Analyze ten properties
- Meet with three brokers
- Make one to three offers
- Tour a neighborhood you're targeting
- Attend a local investor meetup
- Progress builds momentum. Momentum builds results.

## Step 5: Document and Review

Start keeping a simple real estate journal or tracker. Record what you're learning, what decisions you're making, and what challenges you're facing. Your experience will become your most valuable teacher.

Review your progress monthly. Ask:

- What worked?
- What didn't?
- What's my next best step?

## Step 6: Commit to Lifelong Learning

Markets shift. Laws change. Technology evolves. The best investors don't chase trends – they stay curious, adapt, and lead with wisdom.

Make personal development part of your investing journey. Read books. Listen to podcasts. Join a mastermind. Surround yourself with people who think bigger.

## Step 7: Give Back as You Grow

Real estate has the power to transform lives. As your portfolio grows, so does your ability to mentor, employ, house, and inspire others.

- Teach your children what you're learning
- Mentor a new investor just starting out
- Use your income or time to serve causes that matter to you

Success is sweetest when it's shared.

## Conclusion

You now have the knowledge, tools, and mindset to move forward with clarity and confidence. Remember, real estate investing is not a sprint – it's a marathon, built on persistence, learning, and adaptation. Commit to your goals, surround yourself with the right team, and keep your legacy in mind as you grow.

## Your Road Map Forward Checklist

### *Clarify Your Vision and Goals*

- Define your personal and financial goals for multifamily investing.
- Set short-term milestones and long-term objectives.
- Align your investment strategy with your lifestyle and risk tolerance.

### *Develop a Strategic Plan*

- Outline target markets, property types, and acquisition criteria.
- Identify key performance indicators (KPIs) to track progress.
- Plan for portfolio growth, diversification, and exit strategies.

### *Build Your Team*

- Identify and recruit essential team members

(property managers, brokers, lenders, attorneys).

- Establish clear roles, responsibilities, and communication channels.
- Invest in ongoing training and relationship building.

### *Implement Systems and Processes*

- Develop standard operating procedures (SOPs) for core activities.
- Utilize technology for property management, financial tracking, and marketing.
- Set up regular review meetings to monitor performance and adapt plans.

### *Manage Risk and Compliance*

- Maintain up-to-date knowledge of legal and regulatory requirements.
- Plan for financial contingencies and unexpected expenses.
- Regularly review insurance coverage and emergency preparedness.

### *Commit to Continuous Learning*

- Stay informed on market trends, new technologies, and best practices.
- Attend industry events, workshops, and networking opportunities.
- Seek mentorship and professional advice as needed.

### *Track and Celebrate Progress*

- Regularly review financial and operational metrics.
- Adjust strategies based on results and market changes.
- Recognize milestones and successes to maintain motivation.

## Reflection Questions

1. What was your biggest "aha" moment or takeaway from this book?
2. How will it influence your next move as an investor?
3. How has your mindset about real estate and wealth building changed since reading this book?
4. What is your personal "why" for investing in real estate?
5. Write it down and keep it visible as a daily reminder.
6. Based on what you've learned, how would you describe your investor identity today? (Passive versus active, value-add versus turnkey, local versus out-of-state, etc.)
7. What are your top three priorities for the next ninety days in your investing journey?
8. List them clearly and commit to a timeline.
9. What's one habit or system you can create to review your progress each month?
10. (e.g., journal entries, financial tracking, deal log, accountability calls)
11. Who can support you on this journey?
12. Think of a mentor, peer, coach, or investor group to stay connected and inspired.
13. What limiting belief or fear might still be holding you back?
14. How can you challenge or reframe it starting today?
15. Describe a day in your life five years from now. What does your ideal real estate portfolio look like five years from now?
16. Describe it in detail – your portfolio, your lifestyle, your impact.
17. What is the one small step you will take in the next twenty-four hours to begin or advance your journey?

18.   Progress starts with action. What's yours?

# A PERSONAL NOTE

It's been an honor to walk this journey with you. This book represents years of experience, lessons, relationships, and reflection. I wrote it not just to teach – but to empower.

You already have what it takes. You don't need to know everything – you just need to start and keep going. One step at a time, you can build a portfolio that pays you while you sleep, properties that serve communities, and a legacy made of brick, vision, and impact.

The road map is here. Now it's your move.

I believe in you. Let's build something lasting – together.

## Let's Stay Connected

Your real estate journey doesn't end here – **it's just getting started.**

If this book spoke to you, inspired you, or helped you take even one step forward, I'd love to hear from you. My mission is to help purpose-driven investors like you grow with clarity, confidence, and integrity.

## Explore Mentorship or Coaching

If you're looking for personalized guidance – whether you're planning your first deal or scaling your portfolio – I offer a limited number of one-on-one mentorships.

## Invite Me to Speak or Collaborate

I speak on topics like multifamily investing, financial legacy, and women in real estate. Let's collaborate to educate and empower your network or organization. My email is: mellis@fsacap.com. My mobile: 973-216-4181.

## Your Feedback Matters

If this book made a difference for you, please take a moment to leave a review wherever you purchased it. Your feedback helps others discover it – and gives me insight into how to keep serving you better.

## Next Step: Take Action

Choose one thing you learned from this book and act on it within the next seven days.

Whether it's touring a property, talking to a broker, or joining an investor meetup – momentum starts with movement.

You're not alone in this journey.

Let's build wealth, wisdom, and a legacy – together!

# ABOUT THE AUTHOR

**Maria L. Ellis, BBA, MBA,** is a seasoned investor, business leader, and educator with a deep passion for helping others build lasting wealth through real estate. With decades of experience spanning finance, entrepreneurship, and strategic investing, Maria has mentored countless individuals to take control of their financial futures and invest with clarity, confidence, and purpose.

She is the founder of a family real estate investment firm, where she and her team acquire, manage, and grow multifamily portfolios across thriving U.S. markets. Known for her practical wisdom, compassionate leadership, and values-based approach, Maria believes that real estate is not just about properties – it's about people, impact, and legacy.

Maria is also a published author of multiple books on entrepreneurship, wellness, longevity, and women's empowerment. Her writing reflects her life's mission: to educate, inspire, and empower others to live fully and invest wisely.

When she's not negotiating deals or guiding investors, Maria enjoys traveling with her family, mentoring the next generation, and living a purpose-driven life filled with service, joy, and growth.

**Connect with Maria:**
**Email:** mellis@fsacap.com
**Mobile:** 973-216-4181

# APPENDIX A:
# GLOSSARY OF KEY TERMS

- **Cap Rate (Capitalization Rate):** A measure of return on investment, calculated as Net Operating Income ÷ Purchase Price.

- **Cash-on-Cash Return:** The annual return on the actual cash invested, calculated as Annual Cash Flow ÷ Total Cash Invested.

- **DSCR (Debt Service Coverage Ratio):** A ratio used by lenders to assess whether a property generates enough income to cover its debt. DSCR = NOI ÷ Annual Debt Payments.

- **NOI (Net Operating Income):** Income generated from a property after operating expenses but before debt service.

- **Gross Rent Multiplier (GRM):** A rough measure of investment value, calculated as Property Price ÷ Gross Annual Rent.

- **Syndication:** A partnership structure where passive investors (LPs) provide capital and active investors (GPs) manage the deal.

- **Turnkey Property:** A fully renovated, income-producing property sold to investors with tenants in place.

- **Value-Add Property:** A property with potential for increased value through renovations, operational improvements, or rent increases.

- **1031 Exchange**: A tax-deferred exchange of investment properties that meets IRS requirements.
- **Underwriting:** The process of analyzing and evaluating the potential risks and returns of a property investment.

# APPENDIX B:
# SAMPLE DEAL WORKSHEET

Use this worksheet as a quick reference tool to evaluate properties consistently.

| | |
|---|---|
| Property Address | [Insert Property Name or Address] |
| Units | |
| Purchase Price | $ |
| Down Payment | $ |
| Loan Amount | $ |
| Interest Rate | % |
| Loan Term | |
| Gross Monthly Rent | $ |
| Annual Gross Income | $ |
| Operating Expenses | $ |
| Net Operating Income | $ |
| Cap Rate | % |
| Annual Debt Payments | $ |
| Cash Flow | $ |
| Cash-on-Cash Return | % |

# APPENDIX C:
## YOUR INVESTMENT CRITERIA TEMPLATE

Define your "buy box" and stay focused. Fill this out and revisit it regularly.

- **Asset Type**: (e.g., multifamily five to fifty units, value-add)
- **Market(s):** (e.g., Southeast U.S., secondary cities, landlord-friendly states)
- **Price Range:** (e.g., $500,000 to $2,500,000)
- **Target Cap Rate:** (e.g., 6 percent+)
- **Cash-on-Cash Return Goal:** (e.g., 8 to 12 percent)
- **Minimum DSCR:** (e.g., 1.25)
- **Property Condition:** (e.g., light rehab only, no full gut)
- **Management Strategy:** (e.g., third-party PM, self-manage)
- **Hold Period:** (e.g., five to ten years)
- **Exit Strategy:** (e.g., refinance, sell, 1031 exchange)

# APPENDIX D:
# RESOURCES AND TOOLS

## Property Search and Deal Analysis

- PropStream – property data and lead generation
- LoopNet and Crexi – commercial listings
- DealCheck – rental and multifamily analysis
- Mashvisor – market research and rental comps

## Financing and Lending

- StackSource – online loan marketplace
- LendingTree – rate comparisons
- Your local credit union or bank – small multi-family lending

## Property Management

- AppFolio, Buildium – full-service management platforms
- RentRedi – tools for small landlords
- Hemlane – ideal for out-of-state investors

## Legal and Entity Formation

- LegalZoom – basic LLC setup
- Rocket Lawyer – legal templates
- Consult a real estate attorney for customized structures

## Networking and Community

- BiggerPockets.com — forums, calculators, and investor networking
- Local REIAs — real estate investor meetups
- Meetup.com — find local real estate or wealth-building events

# APPENDIX E:
## RECOMMENDED BOOK LIST
## AND PODCASTS

## Books

- *The Millionaire Real Estate Investor* by Gary Keller
- *Rich Dad Poor Dad* by Robert Kiyosaki
- *The Book on Rental Property Investing* by Brandon Turner
- *Emerging Trends in Real Estate* by PwC and Urban Land Institute
- *The Psychology of Money* by Morgan Housel
- *Family Wealth: Keeping It in the Family* by James E. Hughes Jr.

## Podcasts

- BiggerPockets Real Estate Podcast
- Wealth Formula Podcast with Buck Joffrey
- Real Estate Investing for Cash Flow with Kevin Bupp
- The Real Wealth Show with Kathy Fettke
- Apartment Building Investing with Michael Blank
- Diary of an Apartment Investor with Brian Briscoe

# THANK YOU

Thank you for taking the time to read this book. I'm deeply grateful that you allowed me to be part of your real estate journey. Whether you're just beginning or already well on your way, your decision to invest in yourself and your future is powerful—and I don't take it lightly.

I wrote this book with the sincere hope that it would provide clarity, encouragement, and actionable tools to help you take the next steps with confidence and purpose. If even one idea sparked a shift, a new direction, or a renewed sense of belief in what's possible—then it's been worth every page.

I'm honored to be walking this path with you. Keep learning. Keep growing. Keep investing in the life you truly want.

With gratitude,
Maria L. Ellis
Author, Mentor, Investor